MODERN
CHINESE
HISTORY

SECOND EDITION

Front Cover: Jing'An Temple, Shanghai.

Back Cover: Ancient Culture Street (Guwenhua Jie 古文化街), Tianjin.

Key Issues in Asian Studies, No. 11

AAS Resources for Teaching About Asia

MODERN CHINESE HISTORY

SECOND EDITION

DAVID KENLEY

Association for Asian Studies, Inc.
825 Victors Way, Suite 310
Ann Arbor, MI 48108 USA
www.asianstudies.org

KEY ISSUES IN ASIAN STUDIES

A series edited by Lucien Ellington, University of Tennessee at Chattanooga

"Key Issues" volumes complement the Association for Asian Studies' teaching journal, *Education About Asia*—a practical teaching resource for secondary school, college, and university instructors, as well as an invaluable source of information for students, scholars, libraries, and those who have an interest in Asia.

Formed in 1941, the Association for Asian Studies (AAS)—the largest society of its kind, with close to 8,000 members worldwide—is a scholarly, non-political, non-profit professional association open to all persons interested in Asia.

For further information, please visit www.asianstudies.org

Copyright © 2020 by the Association for Asian Studies, Inc.

First printing: 2013. Second edition: 2020.

Cataloging-in-Publication Data available from the Library of Congress.

AAS books are distributed by Columbia University Press.

For orders or inquiries, please see https://cup.columbia.edu

To Wendi, Spencer, Meili and Maya

ABOUT "KEY ISSUES IN ASIAN STUDIES"

Key Issues in Asian Studies (*KIAS*) volumes engage major cultural and historical themes in the Asian experience. *Key Issues* books complement the Association for Asian Studies' teaching journal, *Education About Asia*, and serve as vital educational materials that are both accessible and affordable for classroom use.

Key Issues books tackle broad subjects or major events in an introductory but compelling style appropriate for survey courses. Although authors of the series have distinguished themselves as scholars as well as teachers, the prose style employed is accessible for broad audiences. This series is intended for teachers and undergraduates at two- and four-year colleges as well as advanced high school students and secondary school teachers engaged in teaching Asian studies in a comparative framework and anyone with an interest in Asia.
For further information visit www.asianstudies.org.

Prospective authors interested in *Key Issues in Asian Studies* or *Education About Asia* are encouraged to contact Lucien Ellington, University of Tennessee at Chattanooga; Tel: (423) 425-2118; E-Mail: Lucien-Ellington@utc.edu.

"Key Issues" volumes available from AAS:
- *Indonesia: History, Heritage, Culture* / Kathleen M. Adams
- *The Philippines: From Earliest Times to the Present* / Damon L. Woods
- *Chinese Literature: An Introduction* / Ihor Pidhainy
- *The Mongol Empire in World History* / Helen Hundley
- *Japanese Literature: From Murasaki to Murakami* / Marvin Marcus
- *Japan Since 1945* / Paul E. Dunscomb
- *East Asian Societies* / W. Lawrence Neuman
- *Confucius in East Asia* / Jeffrey L. Richey
- *The Story of Việt Nam: From Prehistory to the Present* / Shelton Woods
- *Modern Chinese History* / David Kenley
- *Korea in World History* / Donald N. Clark
- *Traditional China in Asian and World History* / Tansen Sen and Victor Mair
- *Zen Past and Present* / Eric Cunningham
- *Japan and Imperialism, 1853–1945* / James L. Huffman
- *Japanese Popular Culture and Globalization* / William M. Tsutsui
- *Global India ca 100 CE: South Asia in Early World History* / Richard H. Davis
- *Caste in India* / Diane Mines
- *Understanding East Asia's Economic "Miracles"* / Zhiqun Zhu
- *Political Rights in Post-Mao China* / Merle Goldman
- *Gender, Sexuality, and Body Politics in Modern Asia* / Michael Peletz

About the Author

DAVID KENLEY is currently Dean of the College of Arts and Sciences at Dakota State University. Formerly Professor of Chinese History at Elizabethtown College, he is committed to the concept of the scholar-teacher. Kenley's research interests focus on Chinese migration. His publications include *New Culture in a New World: The May Fourth Movement and the Chinese Diaspora, 1919–1932* as well as *Contested Community: Identities, Spaces, and Hierarchies of the Chinese in the Cuban Republic* (with Miriam Herrera Jerez and Mario Castillo Santana). Currently he is researching Western peacemaking activities in early twentieth-century China.

Contents

LIST OF ILLUSTRATIONS

Figures

Maps

Table

Acknowledgments

I t has been tremendously rewarding to collaborate with Lucien Ellington, Jon Wilson, and their colleagues at the Association for Asian Studies. Based on my experiences with them on the first edition of *Modern Chinese History*, I eagerly accepted Dr. Ellington's invitation to work on this second edition. I appreciate Dr. Ellington's skillful guidance, his collegiality, and his unfailing commitment to the field of Asian pedagogy.

For the past several years, I have benefited from the professional support of my colleagues at Elizabethtown College. As a small liberal arts college, "Etown" is committed to both high quality scholarship as well as first-rate teaching. I hope *Modern Chinese History* reflects both of these commitments and I thank my colleagues for modeling the best of both worlds.

The images in this volume make it much more attractive, engaging, and instructive. Thanks to Matthew Sudnik and Bryan Greenberg for allowing me to use some of their photographs, along with numerous other individuals who graciously share their work in the public domain.

Wendi Carlson Kenley and our children continue to motivate me in all I do and this second edition of *Modern Chinese History* is dedicated to them.

Editor's Introduction

I t It is a distinct privilege and honor to introduce the second edition of David Kenley's *Modern Chinese History*. In addition to developing the initial Key Issues volume, David and I have worked together on several articles he has published in *Education About Asia*, he has served as a referee for the journal on a number of occasions; and as I write this introduction, David is in a leadership position in a collaborative project involving Asia Shorts, another AAS book series, and *Education About Asia*. David has also been extensively involved in the National Consortium for Teaching About Asia (NCTA) professional development programs for teachers. Although an accomplished scholar, and now educational leader with his recent appointment as Dean of the College of Arts and Sciences at Dakota State University, David is especially competent in writing lucid, interesting, and content-rich prose for non-specialists including university, and secondary school teachers, and most important, their students. I have used his earlier edition in my own courses and in professional development programs for teachers and can strongly attest how much readers indicate they learned about modern China and their positive reactions to the prior volume.

David's chronicle of modern China includes ample content on China's relations with the world but does not neglect the many individual Chinese who helped in shaping the country's history. After a brief introductory discussion of the December 2019 identification of a particularly contagious coronavirus in China, and Beijing's response to the crisis that impacted much of the world, David moves back in time to the rise of the Qing Dynasty. He does a fine job of depicting the broad trajectory of Chinese history from China's last dynasty to well into the current era of Xi Jinping. David employs numerous illustrations that enhance the prose.

This volume has already proven to be one of the most versatile publications thus far in the Key Issues series and the updated version will undoubtedly be useful for university and high school world history courses, either as a stand-alone, or a companion volume for Tansen Sen's and Victor Mair's *Traditional China in Asian and World History*. It is also an ideal volume for teachers with little background in Chinese history who are participants in workshops and other professional development on China and East Asia.

This second edition would not have been possible without the helpful comments that assisted in the success of the first edition. Thanks go to Kristin Stapleton who read the original proposal and to Art Barbeau and Alan Whitehead who served as external referees for the original manuscript. Kitt McAuliffe, then a University of

Tennessee at Chattanooga honors student with a deep interest in East Asia, also read the first edition and made helpful suggestions.

Jon Wilson, AAS Publications Manager, played his always indispensable role in the second edition's development. Last and never least, I appreciate the solid support that the AAS Editorial Board and the Chair, William Tsutsui, continually exhibit for the pedagogical publications, Key Issues in Asian Studies and *Education About Asia*.

Timeline of Modern Chinese History

1644	Collapse of the Ming and establishment of the Qing Dynasty
1661–1722	Reign of Kangxi Emperor
1735–1796	Reign of Qianlong Emperor
1792	British Macartney Mission to China
1839–42	Opium War
1850–1864	Taiping Rebellion
1861	Beginning of the Self Strengthening Movement
1894	First Sino-Japanese War
1898	Hundred Days Reform Movement
1900	Boxer Rebellion
1911	Sun Yat-sen Revolution and collapse of the Qing
1916–1928	Warlord Era
1921	Formation of the Chinese Communist Party
1928–37	The Republican Decade
1931	Japanese invasion of Manchuria and the Creation of Manchukuo
1937	Japanese invasion of China
1941	Attack on Pearl Harbor and US entry into the Pacific War
1945	Attack on Hiroshima and end of the Pacific War
1946–1949	Chinese Civil War, leading to the eventual establishment of the communist People's Republic of China
1950-53	Korean War involving China and the United States
1958	Launching of the Great Leap Forward
1966–76	The Cultural Revolution

1978	Deng Xiaoping assumes control of the Chinese Communist Party
1989	Tianamen demonstrations and crackdown
2008	Beijing Olympic Games
2013	Xi Jinping assumes leadership of the state and party
2013	Announcement of the Belt and Road Initiative
2015	China builds military installations in the South China Sea
2020	Outbreak of corona virus in Wuhan, China

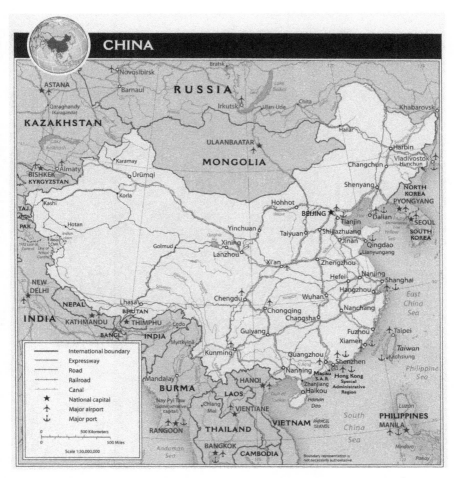

Map of China, showing the contemporary political boundaries and major cities. Reproduced courtesy of the Perry-Castañeda Library Map Collection, University of Texas at Austin.

1

ESTABLISHING THE QING

In December 2019, doctors in Wuhan, China noticed the emergence of a particularly virulent form of coronavirus. One doctor in particular, Li Wenliang, used social media to inform some of his family and friends of the potential health crisis. Screen shots of his postings soon spread across the internet, and local police accused him of making false comments and needlessly inciting social anxiety. They insisted he sign a document recognizing his errors. Officials believed it was necessary to control the spread of information while simultaneously controlling the spread of the virus. Within a month, the number of confirmed illness jumped to over 7,000 people with nearly 200 fatalities. One of those fatalities was none other than Dr. Li Wenliang.

Predictably, international travelers became carriers of the infection and soon cases appeared in South Korea, Japan, the United States, and throughout Europe. The World Health Organization responded by declaring a global health

Figure 1.1. A temporary checkpoint set up to discourage social visits during the coronavirus outbreak of 2020. (Wikimedia Commons: File:刘范村社区走亲访友劝返点01.jpg)

emergency. Beijing officials realized that they were dealing with not only a dangerous virus, but also a potential public relations disaster. In response, they imposed an unprecedented quarantine on millions of citizens from Wuhan and the surrounding region. Business leaders temporarily shuttered their factories and sent their workers home. Consequently, global supply chains fragmented, inventories dropped, and stock markets around the world plummeted. To address the needs of infected patients, China's citizens built emergency hospitals in a matter of days. Soon, stories of selfless heroism on the part of Wuhan's construction and health care workers flooded the internet. Even Dr. Li was posthumously rehabilitated from a boat-rocking agitator to a brave victim who died trying to save others. When international criticism of Beijing's efforts emerged, social media users dismissed such attacks as a form of China-bashing from declining Western powers fearful of a rising China.

In many ways, the coronavirus outbreak represents some of the tensions and trends of modern Chinese history. Since at least the 1970s, China's leaders have focused on promoting economic growth primarily through significant international trade. These efforts reached a climax with China's joining the World Trade Organization in 2001. Since then, China has become a major player in international affairs, exerting tremendous economic, political, and military influence. Today, China is an incredibly cosmopolitan society connected with other nations around the world. At the same time, however, leaders in Beijing have sought to maintain political stability by controlling foreign influence, promoting Chinese nationalism, and highlighting China's unique historical legacy. Textbooks, popular movies, and government publications frequently remind the citizenry that nineteenth-century Western imperialists exploited a weakened Chinese state. Referring to this as the "century of humiliation," they warn the Chinese public to stay ever vigilant against contemporary international slights. China, they claim, is exceptional in the international community.

In order to unravel the multiple strands of modern Chinese history, two main themes serve as organizing principles for this book. The first theme, cosmopolitanism, highlights the role of international, cross-cultural encounters in Chinese history. For many years, Western scholars portrayed China as a closed, xenophobic empire, with the Great Wall as its ultimate symbol. More recently, however, this interpretation has been largely rejected. Scholarship has shown that China has rarely been an isolated, closed society. During the modern era in particular, the Chinese have continuously engaged with their Asian neighbors and the larger world. It is also important to remember that China is a multi-ethnic empire, requiring constant interactions between Han Chinese, Uighurs, Tibetans, Mongols, and numerous other ethnic groups. These cross-cultural contacts have always been two-sided, with government officials, intellectuals, and merchants skillfully interacting with the larger world for their own perceived benefit.

The second theme, Chinese exceptionalism, is in many ways related to the first. Many scholars have argued that China does not conform to widely-accepted norms or patterns followed by other nation-states. While exceptionalism is not necessarily the opposite of cosmopolitanism, it does suggest that China follows its own path, regardless of interactions with other nations. An example of Chinese exceptionalism might be the so-called "Socialism with Chinese Characteristics," meaning that China's path to socialism will inevitably be unique from the path of the Soviet Union, Cuba, North Korea, or any other communist state. While China's history is indeed unique, an overemphasis on Chinese exceptionalism makes comparison and historical analysis difficult if not impossible. This text will identify historical patterns as well as aberrations as they apply to Chinese exceptionalism. Along the way, I will highlight the roles of peasants, soldiers, intellectuals, and officials, including both men and women, as they influence their society and culture.

In addition to identifying the themes of *Modern Chinese History*, it is also necessary to establish temporal parameters. Whereas many scholars suggest that modern China began during the mid-Qing period with the Opium War, others argue that elements of capitalism and other aspects of modernity emerged in China much earlier. At a minimum, it is necessary to understand the cultural and social milieu of the early Qing period to make sense of later eras.

RISE OF THE QING

By the early seventeenth century, the Ming dynasty (1368–1644) was waning in power and influence. Rivalry at the court among civil servants, princes, and palace eunuchs detracted from the daily needs of government and the people as well. As a result, the bureaucracy became bloated and corrupt and the military was ineffective and expensive. Predictably, rebellions erupted near the capital city of Beijing. The emperor, at odds with his own bureaucratic advisers, was paralyzed. Fleeing the rebels, he escaped out the back of the imperial city, climbed atop a hill, and hung himself from a tree.

The emperor's death only exacerbated the chaos of the period. Under the guise of providing stability, Manchus from north of the Great Wall stormed into China, vanquished the rebels, and declared the founding of a new dynasty: the Qing (1644–1912).

From the beginning, the Manchu rulers found themselves governing a predominantly Han population. The Han are the largest, most dominant ethnic group within contemporary China's national borders. They are often referred to as the Han Chinese or simply the Chinese. The Manchus, by contrast, had a different language, culture, and economy. However, they knew they needed the cooperation of the Han peoples to effectively govern. Thus, they soon began portraying themselves as defenders of the Han tradition. They started by providing a proper funeral to the final Ming Emperor and burying him at the elaborate tomb complex of his ancestors. They also allowed Han scholars to staff the bureaucracy, integrating them into the highest levels of government. To this end, the Manchus

Figure 1.2. Ming Tombs in Nanjing, repaired and maintained under the order of the Qing dynasty emperor Kangxi. (Photo by author)

continued the long tradition of Confucian-based civil service examinations. Indeed, the emperor supervised these exams himself and assumed the role of a Confucian scholar. Over time, the Manchu rulers became fluent in Chinese and adopted the dress, styles, and ruling patterns of the previous Han emperors of the Ming Dynasty. To some observers, it appeared as if the Manchu were becoming Sinicized, culturally assimilated as Han Chinese.

On closer look, however, it is apparent that the Manchus retained a high level of cultural and political independence. The military structure, for instance, remained securely controlled by Manchu bannermen, hereditary elites charged with defending the imperial household. Intermarriage among families of top Han Chinese and Manchu government officials was forbidden, and all men were required to wear their hair in the traditional Manchu style, shaved in the front with a long queue in the back. Together with Chinese, Manchu was the official language of all government business. The Manchus also maintained two capital cities: one in Beijing, but the other, Chengde, north of the Great Wall on the Manchu steppe. This cultural bifurcation allowed the Manchus to act as defenders of both Han Chinese and Manchu traditions.

Furthermore, the Manchu elite interacted with numerous non-Han and non-Manchu groups, including Tibetans, Mongols, Uighurs, Russians, and even Italians and English. In each case, they proved to be adept at understanding and manipulating the practices of the foreigners with whom they came in contact. Far from simple Sinicization, the Manchus effectively governed a large multiethnic empire with tremendous cultural awareness. Two emperors in particular symbolize the agility and creativity of the early Qing rulers: Kangxi, who reigned from 1661 to 1722; and Qianlong, who reigned from 1735 to 1796.

THE REIGN OF KANGXI

Kangxi understood the importance of integrating the Han Chinese into his political system. To do so, he sought to impress the intellectual elite with his knowledge of Chinese culture and preexisting political structures. Not only did he preserve the Confucian-based civil service examination system, but he also sponsored the creation of an extensive Chinese dictionary, which remained unsurpassed until the twentieth century. The completed text was monumental in scope. Containing more than forty-seven thousand characters, it created a structure for categorizing and analyzing Chinese terms that scholars still use today. In addition to providing an understanding of eighteenth-century Chinese, the dictionary influenced literature and language for generations after Kangxi's death.

Kangxi also created architectural works that embodied China's cultural heritage. For example, in 1694 he supervised the construction of a palace compound on the northern edge of Beijing. Built on a north-south axis with bilateral symmetry, the complex includes open courtyards, tiled roofs, and decorative motifs common in traditional Chinese buildings. Known today as the Yong He Palace, it is one of the most widely acclaimed and appreciated examples of Chinese architecture.

Figure 1.3. The East Cathedral in Beijing, originally founded by the Jesuit Father Lodovico Buglio in 1653 and rebuilt in 1910. (Photo by author)

Figure 1.4. Macao in 1870. Photograph by John Thomson. (Wikimedia Commons, https://commons.wikimedia.org/wiki/File:Macao,_China._Photograph_by_John_Thomson,_1870._Wellcome_L0055550.jpg)

Besides his preservation and enhancement of China's cultural traditions, Kangxi skillfully worked with other non-Chinese and non-Manchu groups. By the time he ascended the throne, there were already dozens of Jesuit missionaries living in China, and Kangxi's court interacted with them on a regular basis. For their part, the Jesuits were willing to adapt Catholicism to local traditions, especially the Chinese practice of ancestor worship, and by 1700 there were approximately two hundred thousand Catholic converts in China. Kangxi issued an "edict of toleration," recognizing Catholicism and legalizing mission activities. The Jesuits responded by providing their services as astronomers, cartographers, clock makers, and even diplomatic representatives.

In 1689, Kangxi employed the Jesuits in negotiations with the Russians on his northern frontier. Several Russians had moved into the traditional Manchu heartland in the area around the Amur River. Fighting ensued, with the Manchus successfully repelling the Russians. Nevertheless, Kangxi knew that hostilities would inevitably flare up again without a more permanent solution. To that end, he asked Jesuits to compose diplomatic messages and sent them to the Russian tsar, Peter the Great. Eventually, the two sides agreed to the Treaty of Nerchinsk, which effectively demarcated the border between the two empires. Border markers placed in the region included Russian, Manchu, and Latin text.

The mutually beneficial relationship between the Jesuit missionaries and Kangxi's court continued for several decades. However, in 1715, when Pope Clement VI issued a Papal Bull disallowing ancestor worship for Chinese Catholics, Kangxi responded by expelling all Catholic priests from China. Kangxi was willing to incorporate Europeans into his ruling structure, but he was not willing to let a foreign sovereign—in this case, the pope—dictate Chinese policy.

In addition to dealing with the Russians on his northern frontier, Kangxi cooperated with the Portuguese on China's far southeast coast. With a trading base at Macao, the Portuguese facilitated an intra-Asian trade network encompassing such goods as nutmeg, cloves, and mace from the East Indies; sandalwood from Timor; drugs and dyes from Java; cinnamon, pepper, and ginger from India; and silks, woodcarvings, porcelain, lacquerware, and gold from China. Such trade also allowed for the importation of previously unavailable New World crops, including sweet potatoes, corn, and peanuts, which revolutionized the Chinese diet. Throughout Kangxi's reign, this trade continued unabated, and shortly after his death, the imperial court opened up trade to other Western powers, as long as it did not directly challenge the imperial court. By the late eighteenth century, the Dutch and especially the British came to dominate ocean-going trade along China's southeast coast.

Kangxi ruled for sixty-one years, making him the longest-reigning monarch in Chinese history. Because of his proficiency in dealing with the Han Chinese, Tibetans, Mongols, Russians, and Portuguese, Kangxi was one of China's greatest monarchs. Under his rule, the Chinese empire expanded geographically and Chinese culture flourished. The stability and prosperity he helped establish continued long after his death.

THE REIGN OF QIANLONG

Qianlong, the grandson of Kangxi, also exemplifies the early successful Qing ruling style. He, too, sought to maintain Manchu identity while simultaneously preserving Chinese traditions and incorporating non-Manchus into his regime. Like Kangxi, Qianlong was ultimately committed to maintaining control over his multiethnic empire and would only tolerate diversity within limits.

Not to be outdone by his grandfather, Qianlong sponsored the compilation of the Siku Quanshu, or "Emperor's Four Treasuries." Containing selections from history, philosophy, science, and other disciplines, the completed work consisted of over thirty-six thousand volumes and was perhaps the most ambitious such project in history. Qianlong also continued the artistic traditions of his grandfather and personally wrote over forty thousand Chinese-language poems. During his reign, the Yong He Palace complex built by his grandfather became the home of thousands of Mongol and Tibetan monks, functioning as a multicultural monastery and

Figure 1.5. Qianlong in his study. Painting by Giuseppe Castiglione. (Wikimedia Commons, http://en.wikipedia.org/wiki/File:Qianlong11.jpg)

securing spiritual authority for Qianlong in the process. Throughout the complex, all signs were in Manchu, Mongolian, Chinese, and Tibetan, and pilgrims from throughout the empire traveled to the site.

During Qianlong's reign, British, Dutch, and Portuguese merchants continued trading with their Chinese counterparts on the southeast coast. As with the Jesuits, however, these trading networks functioned within the permissible framework established by the Manchu rulers. In particular, all state-to-state contacts were subsumed within the tributary system, which itself was a reflection of official Qing cosmology. The imperial court, it was believed, was located in the center of humanity. Those peoples who were closer to the center were more likely to benefit from the emperor's benevolent influence and therefore would be more civilized. Those farther away, by contrast, would be of varying degrees of civility. In other words, all people could be classified according to their position in the concentric hierarchy revolving around the emperor, or "Son of Heaven." Interactions between those nearest the center (the Manchus and Chinese of the "Middle Kingdom") and those farther away were subject to the consent of the emperor. From these beliefs grew an elaborate ritual in which frontier peoples would travel to the emperor's capital, perform various rites such as the kowtow, offer gifts, and acknowledge

Figure 1.6. Even the signage in front of the Yong He Palace, written in Manchu, Mongolian, Chinese, and Tibetan, demonstrates the multicultural approaches of the Manchu rulers. (Photo by author)

imperial sovereignty. For this they would receive gifts from the court and certain privileges, such as trading rights. According to Chinese records, at least eight different nations regularly sent tributary missions to Beijing.

Europeans, especially the British, failed to understand the nuances of this worldview and its accompanying tributary system. Frustrated by the court-imposed trade regulations on the Southeast China coast, the British government sent a diplomatic mission directly to Qianlong's court, seeking to bypass many of the established protocols of the tributary system. The mission's goal was to establish a permanent embassy in the capital city, another violation of the tributary system. Nevertheless, Qianlong instructed his court officials to treat the diplomats with consideration and civility. The delegation's leader, George Macartney, presented his case, but in the end the mission was a complete failure from the British perspective. Qianlong refused to either allow a permanent embassy in

Figure 1.7. George Macartney. Painting by Lemuel Francis Abbott. (Wikimedia Commons, http://en.wikipedia.org/ wiki/File:George_ Macartney,_1st_Earl_ Macartney_by_Lemuel_Francis_Abbott.jpg)

Beijing or alter the regulations dictating commerce on the Southeast China coast. In 1792, Qianlong sent a letter to King George III explaining his decisions. For the last two centuries, politicians and historians have discussed the contents and tone of the letter. Repeatedly referring to British merchants as "barbarians," Qianlong congratulated the king for his "respectful humility" and his "humble desire to partake of the benefits of our civilization." He then explained that China had no use for British trade relations and that exchanging diplomats was inconsistent with China's tributary system. He also issued a thinly veiled threat to the king, writing, "It behooves you, O King, to respect my sentiments and to display even greater devotion and loyalty . . . so that, by perpetual submission to our Throne, you may secure peace and prosperity for your country hereafter."[1]

For the British, this rejection was difficult to accept. Nevertheless, their other options appeared rather limited, and European events—including the increasingly disruptive French Revolution—occupied the king's attention. The failed Macartney Mission demonstrates not only the apparent unequal power relations between these two states, but, more important, it reveals radically divergent worldviews.

ASSESSING THE EARLY QING EMPIRE

For many years, historians have held Kangxi and Qianlong up as model rulers that symbolize the power and influence of the early Qing. One reason for their success, these historians claim, was their ability to defend and assimilate Han Chinese culture. Increasingly, however, other scholars have shown that Kangxi and Qianlong not only maintained a high degree of Manchu identity, but they demonstrated skill and dexterity in dealing with many different ethnic groups, not simply the Han. While it is true they preserved and created impressive works of classical Chinese architecture and literature, they also skillfully interacted with Tibetans, Mongols, Italians, Russians, Portuguese, and the British. Unfortunately, many of the lessons these two great emperors learned either went unheeded by later rulers or were no longer valid in the rapidly changing world of the nineteenth century.

2

CROSS-CULTURAL CONFLICTS DURING THE QING

As seen in the previous chapter, the Qing emperors remained highly engaged with their non-Manchu neighbors and subjects. Their ruling style demonstrated a willingness to adopt and manipulate foreign ideas to enhance their own power. In dealing with non-Manchus, the Qing emperors skillfully defended their right to rule while expanding their authority in all directions.

By the dawn of the nineteenth century, however, many of the previously used policies and techniques would prove ineffective. A rapidly industrializing Britain was looking to expand its own commercial reach, and China was obviously a desirable trading partner. Even though Lord Macartney failed to establish permanent trade relations between London and Beijing, individual merchants continued to land in China's trading ports. The central government in Beijing tried to limit the influence of these traders, while at the same time placating their desire for commercial exchange.

THE GUANGZHOU SYSTEM

For centuries, the southeast coast had been China's commercial heartland. Blessed with abundant rain, rich agricultural fields, and access to overseas markets in the Philippines, Vietnam, and Malaysia, many Chinese along the southeast coast had become fabulously wealthy. Guangzhou—sometime romanized as Canton—was the most powerful city in this region and home to many of its merchants. To allow for trade, and to control that trade, Beijing designed the so-called Guangzhou System.

In its simplest form, the Guangzhou System sought to regulate foreign trade. Guangzhou was located far from the political center of Beijing, on the fringes of the Chinese empire, and it was the only city opened to Western businessmen. Traders could dock in Guangzhou between the months of October and January, and while in the city they could not fraternize with Chinese women, nor could they study the Chinese language. Furthermore, Beijing forbade them to bring women with them from their home countries, for fear they might wish to establish permanent

Figure 2.1. Foreign trading houses in Guangzhou circa 1820. (Unknown author, Wikimedia Commons, http://en.wikipedia.org/wiki/File:Hongs_at_Canton.jpg.)

residences. All Western imports were subject to an array of duties and tariffs, many of which changed according to the capricious dictates of the local authorities. Most frustrating for the Western traders, however, was the monopolistic structure of the Guangzhou System. Beijing required all foreign merchants to trade with one of thirteen officially recognized commercial firms, known as the "hang merchants." These firms were guarantors for their Western counterparts, ensuring that all overseas businessmen would adhere to the stated rules. In exchange for this assumption of risk, the firms had a monopoly on all foreign trade. When disagreements arose between the hang merchants and the foreign traders, there were no other offices to intervene and mediate. Many Western traders chafed at this restrictive Guangzhou System.

Despite its irritations, foreign traders continued to work within the Guangzhou System. Life in Guangzhou was relatively peaceful and harmonious, with English, Portuguese, Chinese, Indians, and various Southeast Asians traveling through the city. To communicate with one another, they developed a patois of English, Chinese, and Hindi, known today as pidgin. Although the system was not perfect, all participants were able to enrich themselves through commercial exchange. In particular, Western merchants and their customers in Europe had an insatiable appetite for Chinese silks, porcelains, and especially tea. However, they found that the Chinese were not interested in woolen textiles and other Western commodities.

Consequently, foreign traders paid for their purchases in gold an<
Between 1781 and 1810, approximately 1.6 million kilograms of si
Southeast China, causing inflation in the region and leading to We
insurmountable trade imbalance.[1]

By the 1820s, however, this trade balance began to shift. Americans, Portuguese, and especially the British found a commodity they could sell to the Chinese: opium. Manufactured in India's poppy fields, traders could easily transport opium to Guangzhou and sell it to the hang merchants. Although technically opium sales were illegal in China, government agents initially ignored the trade. Over time the amount of opium sold in China grew exponentially. Between 1800 and 1820, approximately 4,500 chests of opium arrived each year. In the 1820s, that number jumped to 10,000 chests per year, and in 1839 nearly 40,000 chests of opium made their way into China. By this time, the government was helpless to check the incessant smuggling operations plying along the southeast coast.

The importation of opium had several negative side effects. Working with complicit Chinese merchants, the foreign traders had succeeded in undermining the structured Guangzhou System, revealing its many flaws and loopholes and demonstrating the relative impotence of the imperial court. At the same time, the sale of opium reversed the previous trade imbalance, and silver began leaving China to pay for this addiction. Perhaps most important, opium had a deleterious effect on public health and social mores. Millions of Chinese were helplessly addicted to the substance. Crime and violence were pervasive in some areas and economic productivity levels plummeted. Even the emperor's own son became an opium addict. The British government was aware of the questionable moral implications of the opium trade but insisted that uncontrollable smugglers were to blame.

OPIUM AND THE WAR OF 1839-42

Fearing that the opium problem was becoming endemic, Emperor Daoguang appointed Lin Zexu as the imperial commissioner for the eradication of the opium trade. Lin had previously been a governor-general with a reputation for dealing pragmatically and effectively with opium in his province. To eliminate the use of opium, Lin advocated a two-pronged approach toward his fellow Chinese: stern punishment for dealers and rehabilitation for opium users. In dealing with foreign merchants, however, Lin was less sure of the correct approach. Therefore, he wrote directly to Queen Victoria in London for assistance. His letter combined both economic and moral arguments, and even thinly veiled threats. He wrote:

> There appear among the crowd of barbarians both good persons and bad, unevenly. Consequently, there are those who smuggle opium to seduce the Chinese people and so cause the spread of the poison to all provinces. . . .

> The wealth of China is used to profit the barbarians. . . . By what right do they in return use the poisonous drug to injure the Chinese people? . . . I have

Figure 2.2. One of the pools used to destroy the opium that
Lin Zexu seized from British traders. (Photo by author)

heard that the smoking of opium is very strictly forbidden by your country. . . . Why do you let it be passed on to the harm of other countries? . . . Naturally you would not wish to give unto others what you yourself do not want. . . . May you, O Queen, check your wicked and sift your vicious people before they come to China, in order to guarantee the peace of your nation, to show further the sincerity of your politeness and submissiveness.[2]

Perhaps not surprisingly, the Foreign Office in London refused to receive the letter.

In addition to soliciting the help of London, Lin took matters into his own hands. In the spring of 1839, he arrested approximately 350 foreign merchants and company employees, demanding that they surrender all of their opium. They did so, and Lin was soon overwhelmed with approximately twenty-one thousand chests of the illegal drug. He ordered the creation of three large pools, in which he combined the opium with lime and then flushed the mixture out to sea. For nearly three weeks, Lin continued this procedure, destroying millions of dollars' worth of opium in the process. After completing the task, he released the detained traders and allowed them to leave the country.

Despite his apparent victory, Lin soon found himself with more troubles at hand. Upon returning to London, the British agitated their government for restitution and revenge. Sensing an opportunity to destroy the hated Guangzhou

System, London responded to the merchants' demands by sending a naval expeditionary force to China in 1840. Aware of the impending danger, Lin quickly reinforced the defenses around Guangzhou, building forts and situating cannons pointed into the surrounding waterways. Unfortunately for Lin, however, the British largely refused to engage his defenses and instead merely blockaded the harbor while sending the rest of the naval force north along China's coast. Over the next two years, British warships seized control of Wusong, Shanghai, and Jinjiang and in the process severed communications between the commercially rich south and the political center in the north. Under pressure from local leaders, the emperor in Beijing determined to sue for peace.

Gunboat Diplomacy and Informal Imperialism

The Treaty of Nanjing, which formally ended the Opium War of 1839– 42, ushered in a new era in Chinese foreign relations. Signed in August 1842, the treaty required the Chinese to pay an indemnity of twenty-one million silver dollars, abandon the Guangzhou System of trade, open numerous ports to foreign merchants, and cede sovereignty over the island of Hong Kong to the British. A supplementary treaty also granted British subjects extraterritoriality within China. In essence, this guaranteed that any British citizen residing or traveling in China would not be

Figure 2.3. Shanghai was a small fishing village at the time of the Nanjing Treaty. It quickly grew to become a major center of international trade and a symbol of Western incursion in China. (Photo by Matthew Sudnik)

Figure 2.4. A twentieth-century memorial commemorating Chinese resistance in the Opium War, Humen, China. (Photo by author.)

subject to Chinese laws, could not be arrested by Chinese officers, and could not be tried in a Chinese court of law. Because these treaties were imposed unilaterally, ignoring Chinese wishes and treating them as conquered vassals, historians often characterize them as products of "gunboat diplomacy." Although the Treaty of Nanjing did not topple the imperial court, and the British never explicitly declared China as a formal colony, it is apparent that London used the pretense of war to secure many of the benefits of imperialism. For these reasons, 1842 was the dawn of "informal imperialism" in China. Unfortunately for China, the Treaty of Nanjing was just the opening scene in what would become more than a century of international humiliation. Within months the Americans and French demanded that Beijing sign similar treaties with them or risk military hostilities. Hoping they could pit various Western powers against each other, the Chinese agreed to these requests. In 1844, China and the United States signed the Treaty of Wangxia and later that same year China and Franc signed the Treaty of Huangpu. Similar in content to the Treaty of Nanjing, these treaties further weakened the sovereignty of the imperial court in Beijing. Between 1842 and 1933, China signed at least nineteen unequal treaties. In addition to Britain, the United States, and France, ten additional countries signed such treaties, including Russia, Prussia, Germany, Portugal, Japan, Italy, Austria-Hungary, Belgium, Spain, and the Netherlands. Most of these treaties, including at least two involving the United States, were signed either as a result of war or under the threat of military conflict. Some of the better-known conflicts include the Arrow War of 1856, the Second Opium War of 1860, the Sino-French War of 1885, and the Sino-Japanese War of 1895.

The effects of these treaties were widespread. Millions of Chinese manufacturers suddenly found themselves unable to compete with cheap imports from the mills and factories of Britain, Germany, and the United States. Soon opium was ubiquitous, and the number of addicts escalated. The credibility of the imperial court came into question, as it appeared powerless to stop the increasing presence of the West. Port cities such as Guangzhou, Hong Kong, and Shanghai became international destinations, enticing traders from around the world.

Besides its economic and commercial impact, informal imperialism effected Chinese culture. For example, many of the treaties stipulated the right to evangelize Western religions. Soon Catholic priests and Protestant missionaries began arriving in China. In addition to condemning such traditional practices as foot binding and childhood marriages, these missionaries built schools, hospitals, and orphanages, thereby ensuring that their influence would be multigenerational. Shanghai in particular symbolized Western culture, with Christian churches and other foreign-styled buildings punctuating its skyline.

THE OPIUM WAR AND INFORMAL IMPERIALISM IN HISTORICAL PERSPECTIVE

When seen in light of its earlier successes, the nineteenth century appears to have been a complete reversal for the Qing court. Whereas emperors Kangxi and Qianlong skillfully managed the Tibetans, Russians, Portuguese, and British, their methods no longer seemed to work in the era of Western industrialization and free trade. The Guangzhou System failed to check the expanding pressure from the West and instead precipitated the Opium War. British merchants resented Beijing's attempts to control them, and Emperor Daoguang was unable to use Western symbols and methods to enhance his own power. Even when he tried to use Western-style diplomacy, as seen in Lin Zexu's letter to Queen Victoria, he was unable to do so effectively.

Nineteenth-century China also provides a unique case study in Western imperialism. Unlike British India, French Indochina, or the Dutch East Indies, the West never formally colonized China. Instead, unequal treaties allowed these countries to secure many of the benefits of imperialism without the associated responsibilities. China's economy, society, and even its cultural systems were laid bare to the unwanted provocations of the British, Americans, French, and others.

Nevertheless, it is important to avoid evaluating the nineteenth-century as an era of Western domination and Chinese victimization. China had tremendous resources at its disposal, and its defeat in the Opium War was as much a function of domestic pressure, which will be described later in this book, as it was a function of military defeat. Furthermore, the subsequent unequal treaties represent China's creative attempts to engage with the international community and learn the concepts of Western law in order to maintain its sovereignty, even if that sovereignty was severely compromised. Although China suffered at the hands of the imperialistic West and Japan, it avoided wholesale colonization as seen in India, Burma, Malaysia, Indonesia, and the Philippines.

As the nineteenth century progressed, some Chinese became antagonistic toward the West, and toward their own government, which seemed powerless to protect them. This antagonism would soon explode in a string of violent rebellions and revolts.

3

Society during the Qing

A ccording to Confucian ideology, Chinese social structures were orderly, peaceful, and meritocratic. During the Qing period, the emperor sat atop this social structure, overseeing his subjects as a beneficent, paternalistic figure. Serving at his command was a staff of well-educated civil servants, who earned their positions through hard work and intellectual acumen. Beneath them, the social ladder consisted of farmers, artisans, and at the very bottom, the merchants. Since everyone theoretically understood his or her place in this hierarchy, China was harmonious and largely free of violence.

In actuality, however, this well-defined social structure never worked perfectly. Wealthy merchants chafed at governmental restrictions. Farmers worked long hours to eke out enough to sustain themselves and their families. Some government officials sought to ensure social justice, whereas others used their positions to enrich their families and ensure their own power. By looking at the various roles played by social actors—including men and women—it is possible to obtain a more complete picture of life during the Qing.

Life of the Civil Servant

Since at least the Song dynasty (960–1279), Chinese emperors had used an extensive civil service examination system to select their public officials. Based on the Confucian classics, these exams were rigorous and, for the most part, impartial. On passing the exams, an individual would be eligible for a government position, thereby assuring himself and his family of wealth, power, and influence. The income of the average scholar-official was approximately sixteen times higher than that of the average peasant.[1] Nevertheless, the examination process was extremely grueling and difficult. Boys would begin preparing for the exam at about five years old, memorizing the Chinese classics at a rate of up to two hundred characters per day, until they had eventually memorized all 431,286 words of the seven classics.[2] During the teenage years, the hopeful candidate would study calligraphy, poetry, and composition while mastering the classical commentaries and dynastic histories. By the age of about twenty, a prodigious student would be prepared to sit for the prefectural level of the exams. If he was successful there, he moved on to the

Figure 3.1. Confucius Temple in Nanjing. Confucianism formed
the core of the examination curriculum and therefore was
perpetuated through the centuries. (Photo by author)

provincial-level exam and eventually the national-level exam. For those who failed
to complete all three levels, they could either continue studying and try again or
enter the ranks of the unofficial gentry class. During the actual examinations, a
minister would lock each young man in a small cell for the duration of the test.
With a single plank of wood functioning as both a bed and a writing surface, he
would remain in the cell for three days, writing incessantly. The average age of a
successful national-level candidate was approximately thirty-five. Obviously, the
opportunity costs of preparing and sitting for the exam were immense. The exams
were open to all men, and there are numerous stories of poor peasants sitting for
and passing the exams. However, since the pass rate was approximately one in six
thousand, only those with access to expensive tutors had even a slight chance of
success.

On taking office, the civil servant functioned as a judge, administrator, and supervisor of the militia. During a typical day, he would hear court cases, investigate crimes, oversee the collecting of taxes, and ensure that public works projects were being completed. To keep the imperial official from becoming too powerful at the local level, the emperor would periodically transfer him to a new locale, thereby ensuring that he could not create lasting political networks in any single area.

At the height of the Qing dynasty, there was approximately one imperial civil servant for every sixty thousand Chinese. Obviously, it was impossible for one individual effectively to manage such a large population. For this reason, the civil servants employed a coterie of unofficial gentry to manage many governmental affairs. Most of these gentry were independently wealthy and came from the same elite class as the scholar-officials. Because they were not officially employed by the state, it was expected that they would siphon off funds from the general population through various means. In local governments cadres of lower officials such as scribes, clerks, and jailers also needed to be paid and often also collected funds from the public "under the table" in exchange for favors. While the gentry class comprised less than 1 percent of the population, it controlled over 25 percent of the wealth.[3] Of course, when such siphoning became excessive, peasants would revolt or call on the imperial magistrate to rein in the offending individual.

LIVES OF THE PEASANTS, ARTISANS, AND MERCHANTS

Scholars have tried to capture the details of life for the average peasant or artisan during the Qing dynasty, but the full picture remains rather elusive. Magistrates such as Feng Kecan and Huang Liuhong left records that provide some understanding.[4] As with peasants everywhere, they had certain predictable concerns, namely, dietary stability and physical security. Natural disasters—such as earthquakes, droughts, and infestations— could be devastating to this group of people. Roaming bandits were also a frequent concern, especially for farmers that lived beyond the protective walls of the city. Nevertheless, during the early Qing period peasants were relatively well off. Farmers readily adopted new crops from the western hemisphere, including maize, sweet potatoes, and peanuts, leading to greater dietary diversity. Low taxation rates enabled peasants to keep more of their produce. The result was a dramatic increase in China's population from approximately one hundred million at the dawn of Qing rule to about three hundred million by the nineteenth century. By the later Qing period, conditions deteriorated for the peasants. Corruption among the local gentry and scholar-officials meant higher unofficial tax rates for the peasants. Tenancy rates and rent prices were also relatively high, especially in the densely populated southeastern regions. As a result, peasants turned increasingly to secret militia societies to protect their interests.

Though technically considered lower than peasants, artisans flourished during the Qing. Textile manufacturing, porcelain production, and various handicrafts

Figure 3.2. Twenty-first-century cave dwelling of peasants
in Shanxi, China. Compared to merchants, peasants had
a meager lifestyle in Qing China. (Photo by author.)

reached new stages of development, and many Chinese products became world
renowned. Producers eagerly sought new markets for their goods, looking abroad
to Southeast Asia and even Europe. The government attempted to regulate the
handicraft industries in terms of materials, prices, and wages. Some historians
have suggested that the development of the Qing handicraft industry contained
the "seeds of capitalism," and if not for the intrusion of the West in the nineteenth
century, China would have experienced its own Industrial Revolution.[5]

Merchants, at the lowest level of the Confucian hierarchy, also flourished
during the Qing. In particular, the area south of the Yangzi River became wildly
wealthy because of the mercantile activities of individuals and corporatized
clans. Over time, thousands of Chinese merchants relocated abroad, establishing
long-distance trading networks between their home villages in China with
such international entrepots as Manilla, Singapore, Bangkok, and Jakarta. The
government feared the growing power of the merchants and created numerous
laws and regulations to limit their conspicuous consumption. Nevertheless, they
continued to prosper. Furthermore, with their wealth the merchants attempted
to purchase the outward symbols of the scholar-official class. Consequently, the
Confucian social order was in many ways turned upside down during the Qing.

Figure 3.3. Interior of a wealthy Qing merchant's home in the Jiangnan area near Shanghai. Although the government sought to curb the power of merchants, they still found ways to display their wealth and power. (Photo by author.)

WOMEN DURING THE QING

As with peasants, it is difficult to develop a complete picture of life for women during the Qing period. Seen as appendages to their husbands, fathers, and sons, many families did not even record the names of their women in their family genealogies. Instead, we are left with caricatures of the ideal woman. For example, massive memorial gates placed throughout China's villages record the deeds of prominent local women, praising their chastity, fidelity, and self-sacrifice. These were the values women were expected to emulate.

Of course, upper-class women were able to exemplify these values, whereas lower-class women faced the harsh realities of survival. Therefore, an upper-class

Figure 3.4. Qing era memorial gates in central China commemorating the virtuous qualities of local elite women. (Photo by author.)

woman would be able to remain celibate after the premature death of her husband, relying on family resources to maintain herself. A lower-class woman, by contrast, had little choice but to remarry and pool her limited resources with a new family.

Perhaps nothing better symbolizes the status of women during the Qing than foot binding. At roughly six years of age, a mother would wrap her daughter's feet tightly with long strips of cotton fabric. The goal was not to inhibit growth but to break the bones and form the foot into a new shape. Using these strips, they would pull the toes and heel downward, forming the foot into a fist-like shape, measuring about three inches in length. Not surprisingly, this was extremely painful and debilitating, and some unfortunate women died from infection caused by the process. Most women remained marginally crippled for the rest of their lives, hobbling about on their deformed feet. It is estimated that as many as 40 percent of lower-class women bound their feet while nearly 100 percent of upper-class women did so.

Some have argued that foot binding is indicative of cultural misogyny (the fear and dislike of women), patriarchy, and control. However, it is inaccurate to assume that all women were passive victims of males. When foot binding was outlawed in the twentieth century, many women fought against the ban and continued binding their feet. As with other forms of physical enhancement—ranging from excessive tanning to body piercing to breast augmentation—Chinese women used foot binding to empower themselves. Women with bound feet had a better chance of marrying into a higher class. Wealthy men preferred women with bound feet since they were unable to work in the fields and therefore were a sign of opulence and wealth. Even lower-class women, who could not afford to restrict their economic productivity, would frequently bind their feet in emulation of the upper classes. Ultimately, the majority of men viewed bound feet as extremely erotic. Chinese women no doubt saw foot binding as a sexually empowering attribute in a society with very few alternatives.

THE TAIPING REBELLION

Despite the government's attempt to maintain harmony and stability, social tension occasionally led to violence. Opium addiction and the outflow of silver caused economic problems. Rapid population growth increased the pressure on arable land. The government was increasingly unable to maintain China's infrastructure, as canals fell into disrepair and public granaries' inventories dropped to dangerous levels. For all these reasons, violent groups sprang into existence, and the nineteenth century in particular was fraught with chaos and rebellion. The greatest of these rebellions was led by a frustrated scholar, Hong Xiuquan.

Hong was from the Hakka ethnic minority community but otherwise had a very traditional upbringing. At a young age he studied for the civil service examinations and showed tremendous promise. As an adult, however, he was never able to pass the rigorous provincial-level exam, despite four separate attempts. During this period of frustration, Hong learned of Christianity through missionaries and eventually began having spiritual visions. In one vision, he saw two men with golden beards. One gave Hong a magical sword and instructed him to use it to cleanse the world of evil spirits. After further study, Hong came to believe that the two men were God the Father and his son, Jesus Christ. Furthermore, Hong believed he was Christ's younger brother, or God's Chinese son.[6]

Hong continued his study of Christianity and eventually gathered his own group of disciples. In addition to orthodox Christian principles, he added new doctrine to the canon. For instance, he preached against foot binding, slavery, and alcohol. He organized his followers into a theocracy and redistributed wealth with the promise to end poverty. The charismatic leader also promoted greater gender equality. Over time Hong accumulated a significant following, and his disciples established a religious community atop Thistle Mountain in southern China's Guangxi Province. By 1850 he had over twenty thousand adherents and access to significant financial resources.

People flocked to Hong's message for a wide variety of reasons. Certainly, his version of Christianity appealed to many people's spiritual sensibilities. Hong accused the Manchus of suppressing Christianity in favor of Confucianism, Buddhism, and ancestral worship. The key, he believed, was to rid society of Qing influence, while simultaneously destroying Buddhist icons, ancestral shrines, and

Figure 3.5. Hong Xiuquan circa 1860. (Wikimedia Commons,
http://en.wikipedia.org/wiki/File:Hong_Xiuquan.jpg)

Confucian temples. Westerners were initially fascinated with Hong, and many predicted the imminent Christianization of China. Hong called his burgeoning religious community the Taiping Tianguo, or "Heavenly Kingdom of Great Peace," and his followers were frequently referred to as Taipings.

Despite the overtly religious nature of the organization, many followed Hong Xiuquan without adopting his religious views. Some were enticed by the promise of gender equality while others were intrigued by the hope of economic egalitarianism. Many Taipings were simply frustrated with the status quo and saw Hong as a viable alternative to their precarious existence within the Qing structure. Educated professionals, disgruntled soldiers, hungry peasants, and various members of anti-Qing secret societies joined Hong's community.

By 1850 Qing authorities were alarmed at Hong's growing popularity. Beijing sent a military expedition to remove Hong and his followers from Thistle Mountain forcibly. To their surprise, the confrontation with Hong's well-armed militia resulted in a humiliating defeat for the imperial forces. After several additional clashes with the emperor's army, Hong and his followers decided to seize the offensive. By 1852 they had captured sizable territories in South China and the Yangzi Basin. The cities of Yuezhou, Hankou, Wuchang, and Anqing all eventually fell to Hong's forces. In 1853, Taiping forces captured the symbolically important city of Nanjing, the fourteenth-century capital of the Ming emperors. Hong took up residence in the former imperial palaces and renamed the city Tianjing, or "Heavenly Capital."

Faced with these defeats, Qing ministers encouraged provincial authorities to raise their own armies and assist in suppressing the rebels. With the promise

Map 3.1. Territories under Taiping control. The striped region represents the area surrounding Thistle Mountain, the original location of the Taiping movement. The dark gray represents areas under Taiping control in the late 1850s. (Wikimedia Commons, http://upload. wikimedia.org/ wikipedia/commons/3/3f/Taiping2.png)

of relative autonomy from Beijing, local leaders responded enthusiastically. Li Hongzhang and Zeng Guofan, for instance, raised their own armies to fight the Taipings, and both would remain major political figures for the rest of their lives. In 1855 the Taipings launched an offensive into North China but were beaten back for forces loyal to the Qing. From that point on, the territory under Taiping control began to slowly contract. In 1864 Qing troops laid siege to Hong's heavenly capital in Nanjing. Residents of the city suffered from starvation and eventually surrendered the city. All of the major Taiping rulers were then executed. Although pockets of resistance existed for the next several years, the Taiping Rebellion came to an effective end with the fall of Nanjing.

Assessing the Taiping Rebellion

Historians have spent many years analyzing the Taiping Rebellion. Some have suggested it was not merely a rebellion but more accurately a revolution. Hong's followers were motivated by much more than simply a hatred of the ruling Manchus. Instead, the Taipings wanted to radically restructure Chinese society.

Thus, such scholars point out, the Taiping movement can best be understood as a prototypical anti-imperialist, anti-capitalist revolution similar to the Paris Commune and other such events in world history.[7] Indeed, the twentieth-century communist leader Mao Zedong characterized the Taipings in this light, frequently utilizing Taiping imagery to inspire his own revolutionaries. However, there were also many exceptional aspects of the rebellion, as Hong and his followers reacted to the specific conditions of nineteenth-century China. The multi-ethnic empire contained numerous fractures and areas of discontent. Overworked civil servants, exploited peasants, and frustrated merchants all represented threats to social harmony. Women, with their bound feet and limited options, found the Taiping promise of gender equality appealing. Although Confucian ideology helped organize Qing society, there were nevertheless several million individuals who felt constrained by that structure. Despite the failed Taiping revolution, it was painfully clear that vast and significant reforms were necessary.

While historians may disagree on how exceptional the Taiping Rebellion was, it is clear that it was devastating for China. An estimated 20 million individuals died in combat or perished because of the ensuing social and physical chaos. It was, therefore, the deadliest war of the nineteenth century, far exceeding the American death toll of approximately 620,000 people in the contemporaneous US Civil War (see table 1). The Taiping Rebellion had political effects as well. Although the Manchu rulers succeeded in recapturing Taiping territories, the Qing court would never recover its former power. Instead, authority devolved to the provinces, to individuals such as Li and Zeng. Even with the end of the Taipings, other sizable rebellions periodically erupted. The Panthay Rebellion (1856–73), the Nien Rebellion (1851–68), and the Boxer Rebellion (1899–1901) all caused additional problems for Beijing, which seemed besieged from every side.

Table 3.1: Death Tolls in Various Nineteenth-Century Wars

Spanish-American War (1898)	10,000
Anglo-American War of 1812	20,000
Franco-Prussian War (1870–71)	187,500
Crimean War (1854–56)	264,200
US Civil War (1861–65)	650,000
Taiping Rebellion (1850–64)	20,000,000

Source: J. David Singer and Melvin Small, *The Wages of War, 1816–1965: A Statistical Handbook* (New York: Wiley, 1972); Donald R. Hickey, *The War of 1812: A Forgotten Conflict* (Urbana: University of Illinois Press, 1989).

As the nineteenth century drew to a close, the Qing court continued to face what seemed to be an unending chain of internal and external challenges. The very existence of the Qing state depended on the creativity and responsiveness of its officials.

4

THE COLLAPSE OF THE QING

ate nineteenth-century Qing society was in desperate need of reform. Nevertheless, there was little consensus on what changes to make. Court officials, local bureaucrats, and public intellectuals all shared their ideas with each other. However, most looked to the emperor and his tight circle of advisers to provide leadership. Unfortunately for the Qing, decisive leadership remained elusive, and by the dawn of the twentieth century, the imperial court was on the verge of collapse.

THE SELF-STRENGTHENING MOVEMENT

Throughout the 1850s, the imperial court allowed regional leaders to expand their military and political muscle in order to suppress the Taiping rebels. Many of these leaders, including Zeng Guofan and Li Hongzhang, were advocates of reform. Following the death of the Xianfeng emperor in 1861, his five-year-old son Tongzhi ascended to the throne. Not surprisingly, this resulted in a political vacuum at the highest levels of the government, and thus Zeng and Li were in powerful positions to influence imperial policy. They also had a reformist ally within the court: Prince Gong. These three, together with other like-minded individuals both inside and outside the imperial structure, launched the Self-Strengthening Movement.

The first goal of the reformers was to strengthen the military. To do so, the government purchased artillery and warships from the West. The resulting Beiyang Fleet was soon the largest in Asia.[1] The government also wanted to produce its own weaponry. In 1863 Zeng Guofan sent Yale University graduate Yung Wing to the United States to purchase machinery. According to some accounts, while on his government-sponsored mission, Yung Wing made time to attend his Yale class reunion and even volunteered to join the Connecticut militia fighting in the US Civil War.[2] His offer was rebuffed, however, and instead he secured the desired machinery, returned to China, and helped establish one of the Qing government's first arsenal factories. Soon arsenals were built in Shanghai, Tianjin, Nanjing, Fuzhou, and Ningbo.

The reformers also wanted to change China's government structure. In 1861 they created the Zongli Yamen, the "Office in Charge of Affairs of All Nations,"

Figure 4.1. Empress Cixi with visiting foreign women. (Wikimedia
Commons, http://en.wikipedia.org/wiki/File:The_Qing_ Dynasty_Cixi_
Imperial_Dowager_Empress_ of_China_On_Throne_7.png)

which served as the court's de facto state department. It was responsible for state-
to-state protocol and for maintaining all records related to foreign relationships.
Over the next four decades, the Zongli Yamen produced an ever-expanding
volume of records known as the Record of the *Management of Barbarian Affairs*
(*Yiwu Shimo*). Staffed with bureaucratic functionaries, the Zongli Yamen never
obtained the status or financial support of other government offices.

In addition to altering the military and government structure, the reformers
sought to develop China's economy. Naturally, they wanted to increase the number
of munitions factories, but they also targeted shipping, communications, mining,
and textile manufacturing as crucial industries. In each of these areas, private
investors provided the bulk of the capital, but the government controlled all
top management positions. The China Merchants' Steam Navigation Company,
Kaiping Coal Mines, Shanghai Cotton Mill, and Imperial Telegraph Administration
all emerged during this era.

Despite these auspicious beginnings, many challenges impeded the Self-
Strengthening Movement. For example, although regional officials and members
of the imperial family often cooperated, there was still rivalry and tension between
the Qing court and the increasingly independent provincial leaders. At the same
time, regional officials often used imperial programs to enrich themselves, breeding
corruption, nepotism, and inefficiency in government-sponsored arsenals and
factories.

Even when the reformists recognized these challenges, conservative individuals within the government frequently thwarted their goals. The most influential member of the conservative camp was Empress Dowager Cixi, mother of the Tongzhi emperor (who reigned from 1861 to 1875) and aunt of the Guangxu emperor (who reigned from 1875 to 1908). At times Cixi appeared to support the reformers. At other times, however, she threw up obstacles. Without her full support, the Self-Strengthening Movement was severely limited.

Perhaps the most significant obstacle, however, was cultural tradition. For instance, if the government had been willing to grant more authority to private investors in industry, competition and profit seeking might have brought about better results. Instead, a longstanding distrust of merchants led the government to retain a tight grip on nascent industries. Even the Zongli Yamen, which appeared to be a radical restructuring of the government, was tinged with cultural chauvinism toward the Western "barbarians." If China's top political leaders still believed the West was barbaric, why would they want to reform the empire to become more like them?

THE SINO-JAPANESE WAR

In 1894 China found itself at war with Japan. By that point, the Self-Strengthening Movement was thirty years old and China, it appeared, had changed dramatically. The conflict provided a concrete opportunity to evaluate the effectiveness of China's reform programs. Known as the Sino-Japanese War, the confrontation centered on the Korean Peninsula. Rivalry in the Korean royal family threatened the collapse of the regime, and both China and Japan were eager to assert their authority over the region. Both countries sent troops to prop up their respective Korean allies, and predictably, fighting broke out between the Chinese and Japanese forces.

At the time, many international observers believed China had the upper hand. The Beiyang Fleet, the pride of the Qing navy, appeared invincible. Unfortunately for the Chinese, beneath the veneer of military prowess, they were ill-prepared for battle. Outdated equipment, insufficient munitions, and a poorly trained officer corps doomed the Chinese to failure, and on 17 September 1894 Japan sent the majority of the Beiyang Fleet to the ocean floor. With command of the sea, Japan was able to transport thousands of army troops to Korea. Throughout the winter of 1894–95, Japanese troops pressed the fighting north through Korea and well into Manchuria. By April 1895 the Qing court was ready to sue for peace.

The resulting Treaty of Shimonoseki granted Japan all of the same benefits enjoyed by the Western powers in China, including extraterritoriality. It also ceded the offshore island of Taiwan to Japan in perpetuity and provided Japan with a huge indemnity. Beyond these tangible effects, however, the treaty demonstrated that Japan was the dominant power in Asia and that China's reforms were woefully insufficient.

Figure 4.2. Cartoon depicting the Sino-Japanese War published in London's Punch magazine, 29 September 1894. The smaller Japanese samurai has taken down the much larger, buffoonish Chinese warrior. (Wikimedia Commons, http://en.wikipedia.org/wiki/File:JapanPunch29September1894.jpg)

THE HUNDRED DAYS REFORM MOVEMENT

In the immediate aftermath of the Sino-Japanese War, China's reformers again ratcheted up the pressure on the imperial court. A new generation of intellectuals, led by Zhang Zhidong and Kang Youwei, rose to prominence in imperial politics. Furthermore, they secured a powerful ally in the young Guangxu emperor. Together they would implement reforms more far-reaching and substantive than those of their Self-Strengthening predecessors.

As viceroy of the modern-day provinces of Henan and Hebei, Zhang Zhidong had close relations with the earlier reformers, Li Hongzhang and Zeng Guofan. It was not until 1898, however, that he made his greatest contribution to the reform movement, with the publication of his treatise *Exhortation to Learning* (*Quan xue pian*). In it Zhang argued that China should utilize the utilitarian aspects of Western learning—primarily those subjects most directly related to military development—while maintaining the essence of Chinese culture. He believed that by so doing China would become strong and powerful without sacrificing its cultural moorings. Unfortunately, leading intellectuals found it impossible to distinguish utility from essence, often leading to superficial reforms.

At the time Zhang was publishing his ideas, Kang Youwei also assumed a leading role in the reform movement. Kang was a traditionally trained scholar with rather untraditional ideas. He opposed conventional marriage, instead advocating for annual cohabitation contracts. He railed against capitalism and suggested that the government should provide for the material needs of its citizens, leading some to claim he was a protocommunist. Most important, Kang believed in the continuation of the Chinese imperial system, and he dedicated his life to its preservation. Only with significant reform, Kang taught, would the Qing court survive into the twentieth century.

In the mid-1890s, the young and impressionable Guangxu emperor became aware of Kang Youwei and began communicating directly with him. Kang's ideas captivated the emperor, and the two of them planned a wide-ranging reform program. Starting in the late spring of 1898 and lasting for approximately one hundred days, Guangxu issued dozens of reform edicts covering everything from the imperial political structure to China's system of higher education and the creation of a modern postal service.[3] Of course, an imperial edict does not necessarily translate into immediate reform, but the optimism of that summer inspired observers from around the world.

Empress Dowager Cixi was not among the admirers of the Hundred Days Reform Movement. Sensing that the young emperor was moving too fast and too far in his broad ranging reforms, which included the creation of a constitutionally limited monarchy, Empress Dowager Cixi apprehended the reformist forces. With the help of her fellow conservatives in the court, she launched a coup d'état against the emperor and placed him under house arrest at her summer palace. Kang Youwei narrowly escaped to Japan. As rapidly as the Guangxu emperor had issued the edicts, Cixi rescinded them.

Figure 4.3. Cixi diverted many of the funds earmarked for developing the navy and used them to rebuild her summer palace, including the construction of this marble pleasure boat on the banks of the palace lake. (Photo by author)

Rebels and Revolutionaries

Although the court appeared immovable, changes were swirling throughout Chinese society. At the end of the nineteenth century, both rebel and revolutionary groups grew in number and influence. Within a dozen years, they would severely weaken and then eventually overthrow the teetering Qing dynasty.

The Boxers, originally from Shandong and Shanxi provinces, believed that traditional Chinese martial arts helped them achieve supernatural powers. Consisting primarily of young men, the Boxers were frustrated with their limited economic opportunities, blaming both the foreigners and the Qing court for their tenuous predicament. In 1900, the Boxers began attacking foreign missionaries and their Chinese converts, killing approximately thirty thousand people.[4] When the Boxers descended on Beijing, the Qing court faced a difficult decision: use government troops to suppress the movement or encourage the Boxers with the hope that their anti-foreign elements would deflect domestic frustration away from the imperial family. In the end, the court vacillated as various advisers could not agree on a consistent policy.

Predictably, the Western powers decided to take matters into their own hands, sending an eight-nation military force to Beijing to suppress the Boxers and rescue the besieged residents in the city's foreign legation district. Japan, Germany, Britain, France, Russia, Austria-Hungary, Italy, and the United States all contributed troops to the cause. As the foreign forces closed in on the capital city, Empress Dowager Cixi fled for the relative safety of western China. The residents who remained behind suffered destruction, pillage, and rape at the hands of many of the occupying forces.[5]

Although the Boxers were defeated in 1900, widespread discontentment remained. Increasingly, Chinese intellectuals came to believe that moderate reform was insufficient. Instead they called for a more thoroughgoing revolution. Sun Yat-sen eventually rose to the top of this revolutionary movement. Born to a farming family in southern China, Sun moved to Honolulu at the age of thirteen to live with his older brother and became a staunch admirer of the US political system. China, he believed, needed to overthrow the Manchu Qing regime and establish a democratically elected legislature and executive president. He returned to China in 1883 and launched his first revolution in 1895, which ended in failure. Sun fled into exile abroad. For the next fifteen years, he traveled to numerous countries, visiting overseas Chinese communities and establishing various anti-Manchu political organizations. Within China, his followers created underground political cells and infiltrated the Qing military.

In the immediate aftermath of the Boxer Rebellion, with her fragile government in disarray, the Empress Dowager Cixi finally sanctioned tangible reform. In 1901 she allowed for the creation of a Ministry of Commerce, a Ministry of Education, and a Bureau of Military Training. In 1905, she agreed to discontinue the Confucian-based civil service examinations. The most stunning change of all came in 1906 when she announced her intention to promulgate a constitution. For many, however, these reforms were too little, too late. Sun Yat-sen, for instance, believed these were the desperate efforts of a tottering regime. Indeed, in the fall of 1908 the seventy-three-year old empress dowager became mortally ill. Her nephew, Emperor Guangxu, technically still the emperor though living under house arrest since the Hundred Days Reform, died mysteriously on 14 November 1908. The next day the empress dowager died. Before doing so, however, she named two-year-old Puyi—great grandson of the Daoguang Emperor and a member of the royal Aisin-Gioro house—as the new Chinese emperor. Not surprisingly, many of the announced reforms never materialized before the Qing dynasty collapsed in the fall of 1911.

ASSESSING THE LATE QING PERIOD

Historians have long debated the effectiveness of the late Qing period. It appears clear that the government failed to enact significant reforms, despite the overwhelming need to do so. Empress Dowager Cixi, as portrayed in many history texts, was a xenophobic, power-hungry dictator who refused to adopt the military, educational, social, and political systems of the West.[6] More recently, however, historians have started to rethink the late Qing period.[7] Perhaps, they point out, Empress Dowager Cixi was a shrewd negotiator facing insurmountable odds in an increasingly fractured and powerless political structure. Possibly, they point out, the collapse of the Qing might have happened much sooner without her strong hand of leadership. Indeed, China did face daunting challenges in the late nineteenth century, including foreign aggression, internal unrest, economic stagnation, and several natural disasters. Furthermore, many Chinese individuals were eager to study the larger world and make substantive changes. Zeng Guofan, Kang Youwei, and Sun Yat-sen all looked abroad for inspiration and direction. Consequently, the collapse of the Qing was certainly not a foregone conclusion. As late as 1905, most foreign observers did not predict the imminent collapse of the dynasty. Despite all the problems they faced, the Qing rulers continued to find at least temporary solutions to each one—each one, that is, until the outbreak of revolutionary fighting in the fall of 1911.

5

THE REPUBLICAN ERA

On 9 October 1911, residents of Hankou were startled by the sound of an explosion emanating from a building near the banks of the Yangzi River. Followers of Sun Yat-sen were using the site to produce bombs when one accidentally exploded. Local police arrived at the scene to investigate, but the bomb makers had already fled. Instead, they found a treasure trove of revolutionary paraphernalia, including weapons, banners, and, most important, lists of anti-Manchu radicals. Realizing that their anonymity had been compromised and they would soon be arrested and executed, the individuals on these lists launched a hasty uprising against local government officials. Remarkably, by the morning of 12 October they had secured control over the entire metropolitan region. Revolutionary fervor spread throughout the empire, and four months later the Qing emperor abdicated the throne, bringing an end to centuries of imperial rule.

Marxist historians describe the events of 1911 as a prototypical bourgeoisie revolution, setting the stage for the inevitable socialist revolution that would follow. However, this age defies a simple descriptor and is in many ways unique in world history. The early twentieth century witnessed innumerable chaotic and transformative events. Politicians, military commanders, and intellectuals all struggled to understand the winds of change sweeping across China.

ESTABLISHING THE REPUBLIC OF CHINA, 1912–1916

Sun Yat-sen is widely regarded as the father of modern China and the founder of the republic.[1] At the time of the revolution Sun was in the United States, living the life of a political exile. When he returned to China, he was treated to a hero's welcome. Four days later, representatives of the various revolutionary organizations elected Sun as the provisional president of the Republic of China.

Unfortunately, Sun quickly discovered that the movement was falling into chaos even before getting off the ground. Although troops loyal to Sun had seized control of vast amounts of territory, the Qing government still refused to step down. Yuan Shikai, commander of the largest and best-supplied Qing troops, was in an enviable position. Both sides, the Qing government and the pro-Sun revolutionaries, realized his support was crucial to their long-term survival. Consequently, Sun and his followers opened negotiations with Yuan. In the end, Yuan agreed to support the revolution, establish a new capital in Nanjing, and negotiate the abdication of the last Chinese emperor. For his part, Sun agreed to surrender the office of president in favor of Yuan.[2]

This marriage of convenience was doomed from the beginning. Although Yuan did arrange the end of Qing rule, he remained reluctant to share his newly acquired influence with Sun and his followers. Instead, he filled his cabinet with his own close associates and ignored the wishes of the provisional legislative assembly. Yuan also refused to move his capital to Nanjing, preferring to stay closer to his power base in Beijing. It soon became apparent that Yuan was more interested in maintaining his authority than in establishing a truly republican form of government.

Nevertheless, Yuan did concede to elections in 1913. To prepare for this event, Sun Yat-sen and his fellow revolutionary Song Jiaoren formed the Nationalist Party, or Guomindang. Campaigning on the promise to curb Yuan Shikai's power, the Nationalists dominated the parliamentary elections. Soon thereafter, an assassin shot and killed Song Jiaoren, and once again Sun fled into exile. Although the evidence remained murky, many assumed Yuan had ordered the assassination. Within the ensuing political turmoil, Yuan disbanded the Nationalist Party and evicted its members from parliament. In effect Yuan had succeeded in securing political and military control over the fledgling republican movement and in December 1915 he declared himself emperor. The republic, it appeared, was stillborn.

THE WARLORD ERA AND NEW CULTURE MOVEMENT, 1916–1928

Almost immediately after announcing his imperial plans, Yuan's political system started to crumble. His sons fought over future succession rights, his closest associates abandoned him, and Chinese provinces declared their independence one by one. Realizing he had overplayed his hand, Yuan repudiated the title of emperor, but by then the damage was done. He died in 1916 of kidney failure with no secure regime in place.

Within days of his death, China descended into political fragmentation known as the Warlord Era. Regional military leaders fought with one another to expand their influence and territorial control. At times groups of warlords would cooperate to form cliques, such as the Anhui Clique, the Zhili Clique, and the Fengtian Clique. At other times they would fight ferociously, with as many as a million combatants facing off against each other. Some warlords sought to maintain the appearance of republicanism, claiming to be protectors of Sun Yat-sen's movement. Almost all of them viewed Beijing as the ultimate prize. Whoever held the city claimed to be the legitimate government of the entire nation. Over the

Figure 5.1. The Sun Yat-sen Memorial in Guangzhou, China. Several Sun memorials exist on mainland China and Taiwan. (Photo by author.)

next decade, national politics became a confusing mess of claims, counterclaims, and civil war.

In part because of this chaos, many intellectuals focused instead on social and cultural issues. In 1915 students and faculty at Peking University founded a journal titled *Le Jeunesse* (*Xin Qingnian* or *New Youth*). Over the next few years, it became the mouthpiece of cultural reform in China. Contributors to the journal most frequently attacked Confucianism as a backward and stifling anachronism in the modern world. In addition to Confucianism, "new culture" advocates also

Figure 5.2. Entrance to Peking University, a hotbed of the cultural debates between 1915 and 1925. (Galaygobi, Wikimedia Commons, http://en.wikipedia.org/wiki/File:PekingUniversityPic6.jpg.)

criticized religion, the family structure, classical prose, and various other icons of "old society." Literature became the preferred weapon of these intellectuals, and soon numerous journals, printing houses, and literary societies sprang into existence. Chen Duxiu, Cai Yuanpei, Hu Shi, and Lu Xun were some of the most powerful and well-known leaders of this vibrant cultural era.

These intellectuals saw cultural reform as a first step toward political reform. Frustrated with the endemic fighting of the Warlord Era, intellectuals proposed various solutions to China's political fragmentation. Most agreed that the saviors of China would be "Mr. Sai" and "Mr. De" (Messrs. Science and Democracy). Writing in *Le Jeunesse* in 1919, Chen Duxiu explained, "Only these two gentlemen can save China from the political, moral, academic, and intellectual darkness in which it finds itself."[3] Beyond Mr. Sai and Mr. De, however, proponents of new culture disagreed on what a new political system should look like. Some preferred a pragmatic, problem-based approach to China's woes, calling for democratic federalism. Others suggested that only all-inclusive ideologies—such as communism, anarchism, or syndicalism—could provide the political stability necessary for China.

The confluence of politics and culture came to a head in May 1919 at the Paris Peace Conference following World War I. During the course of the war, Japan had seized German-held areas in the Shandong Peninsula of China. China, which also participated in the war by sending laborers to the Western Front, believed its victorious allies would intervene and return those territories to China at the war's end. However, the international delegates in Paris chose to recognize Japan's claims. China's representatives stormed out of the conference and immediately wired the news to Beijing. On 4 May 1919, protests erupted throughout China. In Beijing the same university students that had been calling for a new culture were now clamoring for political justice. Marching in front of Tiananmen, they denounced the international leaders in Paris and their own inept political delegates. Although it failed to affect the peace conference, the "May Fourth Incident" demonstrated that China's citizens could be a powerful cultural and political force. Many historians believe May Fourth represents the birth of Chinese nationalism.[4]

THE NATIONALISTS AND COMMUNISTS

After the death of Yuan Shikai, Sun Yat-sen returned to China. However, by that time he was but one among many who claimed political legitimacy. Sun reestablished the National Assembly in the southern city of Guangzhou, proclaiming it the new capital of China. However, Sun's actual authority never extended much beyond the provincial level. He soon realized that if he was going to act on a nationwide stage he needed both a tight political structure and a highly trained army. To achieve the first goal, Sun reorganized the Nationalist Party along the lines of Lenin's Bolsheviks. In order to join the party, all initiates had to swear an oath of loyalty to Sun Yat-sen. At the same time, Sun established an officer training school, which formed the backbone of his new armed forces. Commonly known as the Whampoa (Huangpu) Military Academy, the school provided training in artillery, logistics, and infantry command. Staffed with instructors from throughout China and Russia, the school's first commander was Chiang Kai-shek. Chiang had received his military training in Japan and quickly become a trusted assistant to

Figure 5.3. Chiang Kai-shek inspecting troops at the Whampoa Military Academy. (Wikimedia Commons, http://en.wikipedia.org/wiki/File:5062007131230.jpg.)

Sun Yatsen. Using his position at the Whampoa Military Academy, Chiang rose to top positions of authority within the party.[5]

The reformulated Nationalist Party was not the only new political organization to emerge during the Warlord Era. Many followers of the New Culture Movement were drawn to communism as a viable alternative for China's future. Although Chinese intellectuals had been studying communism since the turn of the century, the successful Russian Revolution of 1917 suddenly made the ideology more appealing. Soon communist study groups emerged in various cities, and in the summer of 1921 delegates from across the country assembled secretly in Shanghai to organize the Chinese Communist Party (CCP). Mao Zedong, a young man from Hunan Province, was one of the delegates present. However, the real leaders of the movement were Chen Duxiu and Li Dazhao, both from Peking University and intricately tied to the New Culture Movement. At the end of the covert meetings, the delegates selected Chen and Li as the cofounders of the party.

Initially, the Nationalists and Communists struggled to influence national politics as the powerful warlords in the north found it easy to ignore them both. Consequently, Sun Yat-sen proposed that the two groups form a united front to eliminate the warlords and unify China. They planned a Northern Expedition, a military operation that would move from the south to the north defeating all opposing warlords along the way. After dedicating his entire life to the revolution, Sun's dream finally appeared to be within reach.

THE REVIVAL OF THE REPUBLIC, 1928–1937

In the spring of 1925, during this period of heightened optimism, Sun Yat-sen died of cancer. Chiang Kai-shek, the commander of the Whampoa Military Academy, replaced Sun at the top of the party power structure and assumed responsibility for the Northern Expedition, which he launched in the summer of 1926. His troops, led by graduates of the military academy, were better organized and equipped than those of China's various warlords. Consequently, they experienced a rapid series of victories and by the spring of 1927 had reached the crucial coastal city of Shanghai. Perhaps because of these initial successes, Chiang Kai-shek decided that the alliance with the Chinese Communist Party was no longer necessary or desirable. Therefore, Chiang launched a massive crackdown on all suspected Communists. Hundreds were executed, and several thousand went missing. The tattered remains of the Communist Party fled to the rural countryside or went into hiding.

Chiang's actions startled many of his fellow Nationalist Party members, and for the next several months there was a leadership struggle between Chiang and his rivals within the party. Nevertheless, by the winter of 1927–28, Chiang had again seized control and was ready to complete the Northern Expedition. The remaining warlords standing in his way contemplated an alliance to oppose him, but mistrust and suspicion doomed any meaningful cooperation. As Chiang's

Figure 5.4. Statue at the Longhua Park of Revolutionary Martyrs in Shanghai. The park commemorates the victims of Chiang's Communist crackdown. (Photo by Matthew Sudnick.)

troops entered Beijing during the summer of 1928, the remaining warlords pledged their allegiance to the Nationalist regime and the Northern Expedition formally ended.

From 1928 to 1937, the so-called Republican Decade, Chiang was the leader of the revitalized Republic of China.[6] He quickly set out to implement many of the political, economic, and social reforms promised by Nationalist Party leaders. His first order of business was to construct a modern capital city. Instead of Beijing, he chose the city of Nanjing, located in the strategically important central part of the nation. In addition to constructing impressive government buildings, Chiang and his associates transformed Nanjing into a world-class city with broad, tree-lined avenues, modern office structures, and public transportation systems. He also created banks, universities, airports, and harbors. Although Nanjing was to be the showcase city, Nationalist leaders carried out similar projects in other major urban centers as well. Unfortunately, these efforts by the Nationalists did not benefit most of China's residents, 80 percent of whom lived in rural farming areas.

Several challenges remained for Chiang and the Nationalists. First, though the Northern Expedition was deemed a success, many of the warlords who declared their loyalty to the republic remained de facto independent sovereigns within their

Figure 5.5. Chiang Kai-shek, leader of the Republic of China, during the ten-year republican period (1928–37). (Wikimedia Commons, http://en.wikipedia.org/wiki/File:Chiang_Kai-shek(蔣中正).jpg.)

own territories. As long as they publically supported Chiang, he allowed them to maintain their own military forces and guide their own economies. Sometimes this independence fostered creativity and development; at other times it impeded the effective implementation of national policy. In addition to these self-governing local rulers, the Communists continued to cause problems for Chiang. Living primarily in the mountainous region around Jiangxi Province, Mao Zedong and other Communist leaders ignored Chiang's directives and instead implemented their own policies designed to benefit the rural peasants. Although it repeatedly tried to do so, Chiang's military failed to eradicate the remnants of the Chinese Communist Party. The greatest imminent threat to Chiang's regime, however, came from abroad.

Like other imperialist powers, Japan had wrested numerous concessions from previous Chinese regimes. Chiang insisted on renegotiating these concessions. Not surprisingly, the foreign powers—especially Japan—were reluctant to do so. Time after time throughout the Republican Decade, Japan meddled in China's domestic affairs with the goal of keeping China weak and vulnerable. As long as Chiang was preoccupied with controlling regional commanders and the intractable Communists, Tokyo continued looking for opportunities to expand its imperialist presence in China.

From 1912 to 1937, China was the stage for a confusing political drama. The leading characters included Sun Yat-sen, Yuan Shikai, and Chiang Kai-shek, among others. The supporting cast consisted of revolutionaries, warlords, communists, intellectuals, and foreign imperialists. Throughout it all, China remained deeply engaged in the international arena. Laborers worked along World War I's Western Front, overseas Chinese communities financed revolutionary parties, and foreign ideas captured the imagination of intellectuals. Despite the confusion, by the 1930s many Chinese were hopeful regarding the future of their country. Unfortunately, dark clouds of destruction were brewing just beyond the horizon.

6

TOTAL WAR

Between 1931 and 1949, China spiraled into an abyss of incessant military combat. "Total war" is an apt description of this period. Defined as the use of all available material and human resources, total war can also refer to attitudes and behavior. For example, some claim that normal rules of engagement and expectations of ethical, moral treatment are unrealistic during periods of total war, and therefore nations and individuals have unrestricted authority to inflict terror and destroy the enemy. Millions of Chinese and others died during some of the most horrible conflicts of the twentieth century.[1] Beginning with the Japanese invasion of Manchuria and continuing to the end of the bloody civil war in 1949, every segment of Chinese society sacrificed and suffered because of these hostilities.

MANCHUKUO AND THE SECOND UNITED FRONT, 1931–1936

In 1930 Chiang Kai-shek was holding his tenuous republic together through alliance making, military pressure, and a degree of popular consent. Many of the old warlords had been incorporated into the republic. Other rivals, most notably the Communists, remained firm enemies of the state. Nevertheless, most individuals were optimistic about the direction in which China was heading.

Many Japanese were eager to capitalize on China's weakness. Journalists, military leaders, and other influential public figures in Japan viewed China as a source of raw materials, a market for Japanese products, and a strategic buffer between themselves and their sworn enemy, the Russians. These sentiments became more widespread following the global depression that began with the 1929 Wall Street stock market collapse. With their incomes declining, many Japanese believed China held the key to their own economic survival. Capitalizing on these sentiments, on 19 September 1931, Japanese troops stationed in Northeast China initiated military maneuvers designed to conquer the Chinese region knows as Manchuria.

At that time, Manchuria was a peripheral part of the Chinese republic. The previous Qing emperors originally came from Manchuria and were ethnically distinct from the majority Han Chinese living south of the Great Wall. Since the fall of the Qing, Manchuria's status relative to the rest of China had remained vague. For most of the period, it was under the control of the warlords Zhang Zuolin and his son, Zhang Xueliang. Since the Northern Expedition, Zhang Xueliang had sworn loyalty to the republic. Nevertheless, neither Zhang's nor Chiang's troops were able to mount an effective defense against the invading forces. By February 1932 the entire region was under Japanese control.

The international community was quick to condemn Japan. The Lytton Commission, sent by the League of Nations to investigate, concluded that Japan's actions in Manchuria were improper. By that point, however, the Japanese had consolidated their control over the region and had created a puppet state they called Manchukuo. Theoretically independent, Japanese advisers and military officers staffed Manchukuo's government. For all purposes, it was a Japanese colony.[2]

Despite the problems in Manchuria, Chiang Kai-shek focused most of his attention on eliminating the scattered remains of the Chinese Communist Party. Driving them from their rural Jiangxi stronghold in 1934, Chiang forced the Communists on a four-thousand-mile retreat—the so-called "Long March"—to an isolated region in China's northwest. The retreating troops traversed some of China's most forbidding terrain while Chiang's planes and troops continually harassed and attacked them. Of the roughly hundred thousand troops that began the retreat, only about eight thousand made it to the final destination in the Shaanxi provincial city of Yan'an. Once in Yan'an the Communists quickly reassembled and resumed working with the local peasants. At the same time, they began waging a propaganda war against Chiang. Why, the Communists asked, should Chiang Kai-shek attack his Chinese compatriots while the Japanese were running unhindered across Manchuria? Impressed with such arguments, Zhang Xueliang kidnapped Chiang in the fall of 1936, demanding that he agree to join forces with the Communists against their common enemy, the Japanese. With limited options available, Chiang agreed and was released from custody. Thus the second united front between the Nationalists and Communists was born.

FIGHTING THE JAPANESE ALONE, 1937–1941

Cooperation between the Nationalists and Communists worried Tokyo. Its entire foreign policy was predicated on a weak and fractured China. Furthermore, Chinese public opinion was increasingly belligerent toward Japan. Many individuals on both sides predicted an escalation in fighting between the two nations. On a warm summer evening on 7 July 1937, fighting broke out between Chinese and Japanese troops stationed near Beijing. Within hours both sides had rushed reinforcements to the area. What had initially appeared to be a minor skirmish quickly turned into all-out war. Unlike the peripheral area of Manchuria, this fighting was in the traditional Chinese heartland. By the end of July, the Japanese military controlled the greater Beijing-Tianjin area, and it appeared to be invincible. Many predicted that the war between China and Japan would be over in a matter of weeks.

After securing the Beijing area, Japanese troops moved toward Shanghai on the central coast. Chiang Kai-shek was determined to defend the city, which served as a buffer for his Nanjing capital. Fighting was extremely severe and continued for nearly three months. In the end the Chinese were forced to retreat but not before losing many of their best-trained troops and commanding officers. Chiang's army would never recover from this devastating defeat. Ironically, Chiang's actions

Figure 6.1. This wall at the Rape of Nanjing Memorial lists, in multiple languages, the number of victims of 1937–38. (Photo by author.)

did win the hearts of many international observers. For instance, although the United States remained technically neutral regarding the China-Japan conflict, many Americans viewed Japan as the aggressor and were sympathetic toward the Chinese.

Using Shanghai as their base, Japanese troops moved up the Yangzi River toward the Nationalists' capital in Nanjing. Humiliated at the unexpected fierce resistance in Shanghai, Japanese troops were committed to delivering a knockout blow to Chiang. Unfortunately for the residents of Nanjing, the Chinese military was in no condition to mount a realistic defense of the city. Instead, Chiang ordered his government officials and soldiers to evacuate and move farther upriver to the west. As a result Japan took over the city in December 1937.

For the next six weeks, Japanese troops unleashed a reign of terror on Nanjing's residents. Under orders from their officers, they rounded up thousands of suspected Chinese military personnel and systematically executed them on the edges of the city. Japanese soldiers roamed the city raping women and girls. Thousands of others were tortured, mutilated, and humiliated in the most barbaric fashion. Many Japanese photographed themselves committing these atrocities. According to the Tokyo war crimes trials held at the end of the war, Japanese troops killed three hundred thousand individuals during this period of wanton violence. Today many Japanese historians reject this number as overinflated, but most international observers conclude that the number was certainly in the hundreds of thousands.[3]

If Japan's troops hoped their actions in Nanjing would convince the Chinese to surrender, they were quickly disappointed. Instead Chiang and his government apparatus retreated far up the Yangzi River basin to the relative security of Chongqing in China's southwestern territories. Meanwhile, Mao and his Communist supporters remained entrenched in China's northwestern regions. By 1939 Japan had secured the eastern seaboard, but the vast interior remained beyond its effective control. As a result, both Communist and Nationalist troops remained free to harass the Japanese occupying forces along the front lines and then quickly retreat into the far west. The war, it appeared, was headed toward a stalemate.

Life for the average Chinese varied according to where he or she lived. In areas under Japanese control, individuals had to choose among collaborating with the Japanese, evacuating to the far west, or simply waiting out the war. Not surprisingly, many chose the apparently safe option of collaborating.[4] Others risked their lives by offering passive resistance or supporting anti-Japanese guerrilla movements. In response, Japan divided the occupied territory into three categories: pacified, semi pacified, and unpacified. For those areas deemed unpacified, they utilized a scorched earth policy in which Japanese soldiers killed all civilians, destroyed all grain supplies, and burned down all buildings. As many as two million individuals died under the "three-alls" policy implemented in the unpacified regions. Many

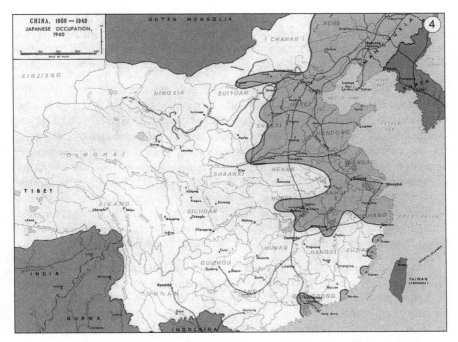

Map 6.1. Territories under Japanese control in 1940. In addition to most of Manchuria, the Japanese controlled much of China's eastern seaboard. (Wikimedia Commons, http://upload.wikimedia.org/wikipedia/commons/f/fe/Japanese_Occupation_-_Map.jpg)

others became war refugees in Nationalist- or Communist-controlled areas in the north and southwest. Chongqing, the Nationalist Party capital, had a skyrocketing population with all of the problems one would expect in such a climate. Inflation ran rampant, housing was scarce, and air raids were frequent. In the Communist capital of Yan'an, Mao and his associates attempted to establish a more egalitarian society by implementing land reform programs and establishing schools for the peasants, all while waging a guerrilla war against the Japanese. In between the three regions—the Nationalist area, the Communist area, and the Japanese area—lay several thousand square miles of no-man's-land in which private citizens did the best they could to maintain a semblance of social order and economic security. From beginning to end, average people simply endured as best they could with a seemingly unending war ravishing their nation.

FROM AN ASIAN WAR TO WORLD WAR, 1941–1945

Until December 1941, most Americans viewed the war in China as purely an Asian affair. Nevertheless, they could not simply ignore what was going on, and increasingly public sentiment shifted in favor of China. Japan, they believed, was waging an unjustified war of aggression, and doing so in a most horrific fashion. In

53

this regard, Japan appeared to be emulating Germany, which in 1939 had invaded Poland and declared war on France and Britain. Sensing the imminent victory of Germany, in 1940 Japan signed an alliance pact with Germany and Italy. From this point on, war between Japan and the United States looked increasingly probable.

Over the next several months, Washington instituted a series of trade embargoes on Japan designed specifically to restrict its access to oil, steel, and other war-essential commodities. Without these goods, the Japanese military was doomed to failure in its ongoing China war. Faced with the choice of expanding the war or withdrawing from China, Tokyo's war planners opted for the former. Southeast Asia, they knew, had abundant supplies of oil, tin, rubber, and other essential raw materials. The only major power standing in their way was the United States. Consequently, beginning on 7 December 1941, Japanese military aircraft bombed American military installations at Pearl Harbor in Hawaii and launched a major offensive against US troops in the Philippines and their supporting naval forces. The war between China and Japan suddenly became a world war.

As planned, Japanese troops quickly conquered Malaysia, Indonesia, and the Philippines in Southeast Asia. The avowed Japanese objective was the integration of these economies into a Greater East Asian Co-Prosperity Sphere, which would lift the living standards of all people in the region. In truth, however, Tokyo designed the Co-Prosperity Sphere to feed the insatiable needs of the Japanese army in China.[5] The sooner Japan could consolidate its victories and end the war in China, the sooner it could negotiate a peaceful settlement with the United States. Unfortunately for Japan, time was not on its side.

Throughout the early 1940s, the United States and China fought as allies against the Japanese. In actual practice, however, the alliance was never a comfortable one. Washington repeatedly accused Chiang Kai-shek of embezzling funds earmarked for the war. Chiang did not have confidence in his US advisers, who seemed to care more about the war in Europe and refused to heed the counsel of Chinese military officers.[6] As a result, the two nations fought independently of one another, as the antagonism and mistrust increased. American military forces waged an island-hopping campaign in the western Pacific, and Chinese soldiers continued to harass Japanese forces stationed in China. Throughout the war, a large portion of Japanese military personnel remained in China with only a fraction facing US troops to the east.

By 1945 the Japanese were becoming increasingly desperate. American forces had seized control of Kwajalein, Tinian, Iwo Jima, and other strategically vital islands. Using them as airfields, US pilots bombed Japanese cities with impunity. On 6 August 1945, the crew of the *Enola Gay* took off from Tinian and dropped an atomic bomb on Hiroshima, Japan. Three days later Nagasaki suffered a similar fate. Sensing the inevitable, Japan announced its unconditional surrender.

Historians have long debated the relative roles of Mao's communist fighters and Chiang's Nationalist soldiers in the war against Japan. Most orthodox accounts

Figure 6.2. The Japanese attack on Pearl Harbor, December 7, 1941. (Wikimedia Commons, http://en.wikipedia.org/wiki/File:USS_Arizona_sinking_2a.jpg.)

written by Western and Chinese scholars tend to emphasize the daring exploits of the communists while simultaneously accusing Chiang of either incompetence or cowardice. More recently, however, a new interpretation is emerging. Chiang, they point out, faced an extremely formidable enemy that until 1941 was supported by Western industrialists. In contrast to the Japanese, Chiang's forces were cut off from external supplies and yet still achieved significant military victories. When the Americans did eventually ally themselves with China, U.S. military advisors severely underestimated Japan's prowess while treating their Chinese counterparts with arrogant contempt. Consequently, both the Nationalists as well as the Communists should be recognized for their accomplishments despite overwhelming obstacles.[7]

At the end of the war, nearly three million Japanese soldiers and civilians were in China.[8] Both the Nationalists and the Communists quickly attempted to secure their weapons and other vital war materials while keeping the other from doing so. Rather than simply seizing their weapons, some Chinese generals incorporated Japanese troops into their own ranks. The United States and the Soviet Union also became involved, assisting their respective Chinese allies in their postwar race for influence. Even before the dust had settled, new battle lines were emerging in China.

COLLAPSE OF THE UNITED FRONT, 1945–1949

Both the Communists and the Nationalists claim to have engaged in the most battles and suffered the most casualties against their former Japanese enemies. Regardless of these conflicting claims, both sides faced tremendous difficulties in the immediate aftermath of World War II. Japan had annihilated Chiang Kai-shek's best troops, and his remaining forces were hopelessly overextended. Mao

Figure 6.3. Mao Zedong stood atop this structure, Tiananmen Gate,
to declare the founding of the People's Republic of China
on 1 October 1949. (Photo by Bryan Greenberg.)

Zedong's Communists had a fraction of the heavy artillery, tanks, and airplanes their Nationalist rivals possessed. However, more important than troop strength was the crucial battle for public opinion. This was most evident in the battle for Manchuria.

Manchuria had been under Japanese control since 1931. Japanese military and business leaders had invested heavily in the region's industrial base. Both the Nationalists and the Communists knew of its strategic and material importance. Both sides rushed personnel to the area to fill the resulting vacuum as Japanese returned to their home islands. Within a few months, Nationalist troops had gained control of nearly all the major cities. However, Communist troops were widespread in the surrounding countryside. Rural peasants responded favorably to the land reform and educational policies implemented by the Communists. Urban residents, by contrast, suffered from the widespread inflation, corruption, and bureaucratic inefficiencies that plagued Chiang Kai-shek's government. Consequently, the rural peasants were more willing to sacrifice for the support of the Communists, whereas members of the urban middle class were much less willing to defend the Nationalists. Soon the Nationalist troops in Manchuria found themselves isolated in their cities surrounded by hostile forces. Predictably, Manchuria quickly fell into Communist hands.

Even while the battle was raging in Manchuria, U.S. President Harry Truman sent General George C. Marshall to negotiate a peaceful settlement between the two sides. The United States was providing massive economic and military aid to the Nationalists, and therefore Marshall had some leverage in dealing with Chiang Kai-shek. The Communists, by contrast, were not indebted to Washington. As time progressed, Chiang increasingly appeared to be a puppet figure of the United States. Despite his best attempts to win the trust of both sides, the talks broke down and Marshall returned to the United States in January 1947.

The next eighteen months witnessed an almost unbroken string of Communist victories in the war.[9] Often Nationalist commanders would simply switch sides, bringing with them both their troops and their equipment. Peasants, motivated by the promise of land reform, flocked to the Communist cause, and soon Mao's troops vastly outnumbered Chiang's. Chiang responded by using the same tactics that worked in fighting the Japanese: he retreated to the western interior. By 1949, however, even that isolated region appeared vulnerable, and Chiang started relocating his government apparatus to the relatively safe offshore island of Taiwan, which had only recently returned from Japanese to Chinese control. On 1 October 1949, Mao stood atop the Tiananmen Gate in Beijing and announced the establishment of the People's Republic of China. After more than a century of invasion and international humiliation, Mao explained, the Chinese people had finally "stood up."

Figure 6.4. The Chiang Kai-shek Memorial Hall
in Taipei, Taiwan. (Photo by author.)

With his troops and supporters in Taiwan, Chiang hoped to buy a little time, rally international support, and resume fighting against the Communists. In actuality, the civil war was over. Although Chiang would continue to rule Taiwan until his death in 1975, he would never return to the mainland. Instead an ambiguous peace settled in between the two sides, with each looking forward to the day of eventual reunification. Today the Nationalist Party remains one of two leading parties in the sovereign state of the Republic of China, which is still located on the island of Taiwan.

Total War is a fitting description for the era extending from 1931 to 1949. Not only did the Chinese and Japanese utilize all available resources in waging war, but the period also witnessed horrific acts of violence, such as the Rape of Nanjing, which violated all acceptable rules of engagement. In the end approximately 15 to 20 million Chinese died as a result of the war with Japan, and an additional 2.5 million died in the subsequent civil war.[10] As Mao explained, the Chinese people had finally "stood up," but there was a lot of healing to do for the new Communist state. The trauma and destruction of these violent years would last for decades.

7

The Turbulent 1950s and 1960s

When Mao declared the founding of the People's Republic in 1949, the nation was facing innumerable challenges. Widespread destruction from nearly two decades of war, rampant inflation, and international isolation were only a few of the problems Mao and his associates confronted. Yet within a few short years, the Chinese Communist Party recorded some rather remarkable achievements and earned the goodwill of the people. Unfortunately, the turbulence that accompanied the Great Leap Forward of the late 1950s and the Cultural Revolution of the 1960s reversed this positive trend. Thus, the story of the People's Republic for this period is one of hope followed by tragedy.

Establishing a New Society

The first order of business for the new political regime was economic reform. Runaway inflation caused by war and government fiscal mismanagement had destroyed the economies of China's urban centers. To check this problem, the central government created a new currency and eliminated much of the money in circulation. Within a year inflation was gone. Beyond currency reform, Mao and his advisers largely left the urban economy untouched. Instead they implemented an aggressive propaganda campaign designed to reassure the urban elite and win their loyalty. Nevertheless, foreign-owned businesses began withdrawing from China.

By contrast, the situation in the countryside was nothing short of revolutionary. In 1950 Beijing passed the Agrarian Reform Law. Designed to confiscate land from wealthy landowners and redistribute it to poor farmers, the law affected nearly 60 percent of the total population. Nevertheless, the government found it difficult to implement it. Local party cadres simply did not have the military strength to confiscate land by force. Instead, they studied local social structures and incited landless peasants to implement reform of their own accord. Time after time in villages across China, poor families stormed the homes of local elites demanding they surrender their land deeds. Sometimes these well-connected property owners resisted, resulting in small-scale battles. In the end historians estimate that as many as one million individuals were killed in this ongoing process.

By 1953, officials had successfully implemented the Agrarian Reform Law and Mao believed it was the appropriate time to encourage land collectivization. Peasants were initially urged to pool their resources— including livestock, capital equipment, and labor—into collectively farmed properties. Theoretically, each farmer still owned his own land, but he worked it together with others. Eventually, the government encouraged farmers to sign over their land deeds to a collective entity, officially surrendering private ownership. By the mid-1950s there were hundreds of thousands of collectivized farms across China. Some of them involved several hundred individuals each.

At the same time the government was implementing these reforms, it was facing an international crisis. In 1949, Chiang Kai-shek and his supporters had fled to the offshore island of Taiwan. However, the two sides never officially declared an end to the civil war. Therefore, the international community was forced to recognize either Mao's regime in Beijing or Chiang's in Taiwan. The United States continued to recognize Chiang, yet many Washington insiders were arguing for the opposite. In 1950 these arguments became moot when communist North Korea invaded pro-American South Korea. Under United Nations auspices, US president Harry Truman sent troops to shore up South Korea's defenses, with troops landing at Inchon in September. The next month China responded by sending its own troops into the conflict in support of the North. Suddenly the United States and China, former allies in the war against Japan, found themselves fighting each other on the Korean Peninsula. For obvious reasons, the United States decided not to recognize the government in Beijing and to maintain relations with Chiang. Most of America's allies followed suit.

The Korean War could have been disastrous for the fledgling People's Republic. Indeed, the US military was the most powerful in the world. Nevertheless, Mao convinced his people that America was a "paper tiger," ferocious looking but with no substance. He sent millions of Chinese to the Korean front with little military training and inadequate supplies. Their sheer numbers, however, often overwhelmed young American GIs. After three years of bitter fighting, the belligerents agreed to a cease-fire, recognizing an effective stalemate between the North and the South. Although the numbers are still debated, an estimated four hundred thousand Chinese died in the war. Nevertheless, Beijing had demonstrated that it would not back down in the face of the paper tiger. Any hopes of reconciliation between China and the United States were dashed for the next generation.

By the mid-1950s the Chinese Communist Party appeared to be riding a long string of successes. Having conquered inflation, reformed landholding, and faced down the United States on the battlefield, Mao and his associates were feeling confident. Perhaps because of this, in 1957 Mao invited the citizenry to publicly speak out and offer evaluations of the party and its first few years in power. Known as the Hundred Flowers Campaign (based on an old Confucian phrase), this period of political openness proved to be short-lived. Intellectuals in particular

Figure 7.1. Chinese troops crossing the frozen Yalu River on their way to the battlefields in Korea. (Wikimedia Commons, http://en.wikipedia.org/wiki/File:China_Crosses_Yalu.jpg.)

responded to Mao's invitation and publicly criticized both Mao and his party. Almost as quickly as it began, Mao clamped down on this dissent, launching the Anti-rightists Campaign of 1957. Thousands of individuals who had responded to the call for critique suddenly found themselves in labor camps and prisons. Perhaps the most famous of these prisons was Jiabiangou in the desert region of China's Gansu Province. Recently historians have become aware of the heart-wrenching tales of starvation and deprivation within these prisons.[1] Many others waited patiently for word of their loved ones locked away at Jiabiangou and similar institutions. For many cynics it appeared as though Mao had deceitfully laid a trap for his enemies. Despite the relative successes of the first few years, trust between the party and the people was starting to show signs of stress.

THE GREAT LEAP FORWARD

With the success of land reform and collectivization, the Communist Party leadership was prepared to initiate a Great Leap Forward in 1958.[2] Mao called for the thousands of collective farms to merge into communes. These became massive agricultural associations, consisting of approximately twenty-five thousand individuals each and functioning as self-sustaining communist communities. Each commune had its own public canteen, or cafeteria, in which all members were fed. Communes also contained schools, infirmaries, and nursing homes. Theoretically, by working together the commune members would be able to produce more food than they collectively needed, allowing the government to skim off the excess to feed urban workers and sell in the international market. By the end of 1958, the vast majority of the farming population lived on a commune. In a nation where 80 percent of the total population lived in rural areas, approximately half a billion men, women, and children lived in communes.

Despite its agricultural elements, the real goal of the Great Leap Forward was to enhance industrial output in electricity, coal, and especially steel. Mao challenged China to surpass Britain in steel production within fifteen years, and workers responded with great enthusiasm and optimism. Mao believed that sheer willpower determined reality and was the key to accomplishing this goal, regardless of infrastructure or training. In fact Mao frequently belittled those who offered excuses, claiming they were simply ideologically impure or deluded by capitalist claims. He promoted those who adhered to his line and purged those who pointed out inconvenient scientific truths. As a result, many agricultural and industrial schemes were doomed to failure. The paramount symbol of such misplaced optimism was the shoddily constructed "backyard furnace." Men, women, and children would collect various tools and implements such as pots, hammers, and bicycles and smelt them in these small blast furnaces to create pig iron. Naturally, these were not high quality furnaces, and their operators knew nothing about manufacturing steel. However, they believed that willpower was superior to quality control. Therefore, output increased but the inferior iron was useless. Farmers used similarly nonsensical methods in agricultural production, such as deep planting and positioning seedlings too close together, which drastically reduced agricultural yields.

In 1959 the Great Leap Forward turned disastrous. Fearful of Mao and other central government officials, many local and midlevel party leaders inflated production figures and over-reported agricultural yields. The central government responded by requisitioning the "surplus" grain and setting even higher goals for the next harvest. As a result many communes did not have sufficient grain supplies to feed their own people. Referred to as the "three lean years," the period from 1959 to 1961 witnessed the starvation of approximately thirty million Chinese, more than had died in the war against Japan. It was the largest man-made famine in the history of the world. Today the Great Leap Forward famine remains a taboo subject for historians operating within China, and state records are still closed to researchers. Consequently, Western scholars can only guess at the levels of suffering endured by millions of Chinese peasants and families.

THE CULTURAL REVOLUTION

Because of the disastrous Great Leap Forward, by the end of the 1950s Mao's grip on leadership was slipping away. In July 1959 party leaders gathered for a series of high-level meetings. Before adjourning several days later, they had forced Mao to relinquish his position as head of state and replaced him with Liu Shaoqi. Liu quickly began reversing many of Mao's policies, including dismantling

Figure 7.2. "Backyard furnaces" used to smelt iron during
the Great Leap Forward. (Wikimedia Commons,
http://en.wikipedia.org/wiki/File:Backyard_furnace4.jpg.)

the commune system. Together with one of his party allies, Deng Xiaoping, Liu
Shaoqi instituted a range of reforms designed to reintroduce market forces into
the economy. These reforms quickly made an impact on production, helping to
end the massive starvation of the Great Leap Forward. Between 1960 and 1966,
China's economy stabilized and a sense of normalcy returned to both the cities
and the countryside.

By this time Mao was already well into his sixties. He had spent his entire
adult life fighting for a communist revolution, and in his twilight years he was
watching it unravel at the hands of his party rivals. He naturally did not simply
want to watch Liu, Deng, and various other "capitalist roaders" turn China away
from a communist revolution. Nevertheless, Mao had been stripped of many of his
formal positions. Reinvigorating the revolution, he realized, would require use of
the extralegal weapons he still wielded. For instance, despite the disastrous Great
Leap Forward, Mao was still widely revered as the liberator of China and the father

of the People's Republic. At a minimum such adoration enabled him to enlist the support of millions of followers as he struck back at his political rivals.

In 1966 Mao launched what he called the Great Proletarian Cultural Revolution. Traitors had infiltrated the party, he warned, and an army of volunteers was required to root them out. He specifically challenged China's youth to respond to his call. Millions of teenagers and young adults formed themselves into paramilitary groups, or Red Guards, donning makeshift uniforms and red armbands.[3] There were many reasons why youths chose to participate in this movement. Some were revolutionary idealists longing for adventure. Others were seeking to prove their loyalty and distance themselves from questionable counterrevolutionary ties. Still others joined because of peer pressure or in response to the threat of force. Regardless of their motives, Red Guard groups targeted suspected counterrevolutionaries within their schools and communities. Once they apprehended such individuals, the vigilante youths would hold public "trials" of the accused, often forcing them to participate in humiliating public spectacles. Any type of evidence could be used to prove counterrevolutionary tendencies, ranging from the possession of Western books and music to insufficient displays of communist enthusiasm.

During the ensuing years, millions were removed from their positions, forced into labor camps, or sent to reeducation facilities to reestablish their revolutionary credentials. As expected, Liu Shaoqi ended up in prison, where he died shortly thereafter from untreated diabetes. Liu's political ally, Deng Xiaoping, was sent to work in the countryside. Besides these two, revolutionary zealots publically persecuted thousands of individuals from all walks of life, many of whom committed suicide rather than face their teenage accusers.

Throughout the Cultural Revolution, devotion to Mao was the primary indicator of an individual's revolutionary fervor. Consequently, Mao worship reached almost cult like status. Red Guards carried copies of Mao's "Little Red Book," which contained his words of wisdom about life and revolution. Mothers and fathers filled their homes with Mao statues, posters, and other decorative items. Nearly everybody wore and collected millions of pins displaying Mao's image. The masses referred to him as the "Great Helmsman" and the "Reddest-red Sun of Our Hearts." Propaganda posters portrayed him in godlike poses with radiant beams protruding from his head. For his part Mao fostered such adoration, greeting adoring crowds and encouraging their mass devotion. By 1971 he had eliminated all of his rivals, and he was once again the unquestioned leader of the Communist Party.

Unfortunately for Mao, it was much easier to whip up revolutionary fervor among the young than to harness it. Once he had succeeded in eliminating his rivals, Mao turned his attention to calming the Red Guard storm. He did this by using their own commitment and devotion against them. Under the guise of the "Down to the Countryside" movement, Mao appealed to urban youth to move

Figure 7.3. President Richard Nixon meeting with Mao Zedong in China during the height of the Cultural Revolution, 1972. (Wikimedia Commons, http://en.wikipedia.org/wiki/File:Nixon_Mao_1972-02-29.png.)

to remote rural areas to spread the revolutionary message. Millions responded to his call, traveling to Inner Mongolia, Tibet, and other remote locations. Soon, however, harsh realities tempered their enthusiasm. Many found they were not physically capable of handling the rigors of farm work. Others were hopelessly homesick and felt trapped in their new situations. Local residents resented the arrival of these urban teenagers with their sense of superiority and lack of useful skills. Within a few years, many young men and women began to understand their own roles as pawns in Mao's political power struggle.

Interestingly, it was in the midst of the Cultural Revolution that the United States and the People's Republic of China began the dance of rapprochement. In 1971 US national security adviser Henry Kissinger, with the authorization of President Richard Nixon, secretly traveled to China to meet with Communist Party officials. The next year, Nixon made a similar trip and personally met with Mao Zedong. Because of Nixon's previously harsh criticisms of communism, the meeting shocked the world. As a result of their deliberations, the two sides issued the "Shanghai Communiqué," paving the way for the eventual normalization of relations between Beijing and Washington.

In 1976 Mao died of natural causes, bringing a formal end to the Cultural Revolution. For the next few days, there was a power struggle within the party. In the end most of Mao's main political allies were rounded up and thrown into prison, including his wife, Jiang Qing, and the other members of her so-called Gang of Four. The Chinese courts convicted them of persecuting to death 34,800 people and injuring an additional 729,511. In truth perhaps as many as 100 million Chinese suffered because of the ten-year reign of madness. Party leaders quietly began pulping Mao's "Little Red Book" and removing his image from public display. Most Chinese, it seemed, were eager to put the Cultural Revolution into the past. Today most Chinese unhesitatingly characterize the Cultural Revolution as an unmitigated disaster. The youths of this era remain undereducated relative to both their seniors and their juniors, leading to what some call the "lost generation" of China. Zealous Red Guards vandalized and destroyed hundreds of thousands of homes, temples, and historical sites. It took several years for the economy to regain its footing, and the credibility of the party fell in the eyes of almost everyone.

Historians remain fascinated with the Cultural Revolution. Mao used the movement to enhance his power, leading to his own deification. Yet it is too easy to blame Mao alone for these ten years of chaos.[4] For much of the period, Mao played a passive role as a public icon. Many political elites were eager to exploit Mao's status to enhance their own power. Furthermore, millions of Red Guards and other seemingly normal individuals throughout Chinese society willingly participated.[5] Historians are interested in understanding the motives, methods, and expectations of these revolutionaries. In the years following Mao's death, many individuals published memoirs recounting their suffering during the Cultural Revolution. Known as "scar literature," these stories depict in graphic detail the heroic acts of love and compassion many individuals displayed during this dark era. More recently former Red Guards have published their own memoirs, shedding light on their intentions and influences. Using these works of literature, historians are increasingly able to understand the impact of the Cultural Revolution on the common men and women of this divisive period.

Between 1949 and 1976, the People's Republic of China struggled to establish a new socialist society. Despite their initial successes, party leaders soon faced massive famines and public chaos. Mao Zedong, the most recognizable individual of this era, remains a controversial figure to this day, with some hailing him as a patriotic liberator and others vilifying him as a cruel megalomaniac. Nevertheless, it is important to remember the stories of thousands of ordinary people affected by the Hundred Flowers Movement, the Great Leap Forward, and the Cultural Revolution. For millions of Chinese men, women, and children, this was a truly revolutionary era.

8

THE POST-MAO ERA

Mao Zedong played the dominant role in Chinese history from 1949 to 1976, a period of unending revolution and chaos. By contrast, several individuals have guided China during the post-Mao era, a period of relative stability. Nevertheless, since 1976 China has experienced a remarkable transformation that is nothing short of revolutionary. Deng Xiaoping's pragmatic leadership style, which his successors have copied, dramatically improved the lives of China's billion-plus residents. At the same time, China today is intricately tied to the international community and governments from around the globe are studying China's keys to development. Of course, there are still many intractable problems facing China as its citizens navigate the rapidly changing environment of the twenty-first century.

DENG XIAOPING AND THE FOUR MODERNIZATIONS

Predictably, Mao's death in 1976 led to a leadership vacuum at the apex of the Communist Party. Most Chinese could not remember life before Mao. Two main groups stood ready to resume the mantle of leadership: those who wished to continue Mao's policies and those who were eager for reform. Behind closed doors, these two groups wrangled over party policies and patronage. By 1978 the reformers had gained the upper hand. Ironically, a man that was the target of Mao's Cultural Revolution—Deng Xiaoping—emerged as the most powerful individual in the party and the state apparatus.[1]

Before the Cultural Revolution, Deng Xiaoping's revolutionary credentials were impeccable. Born to a peasant family in 1904, Deng studied Marxism in the 1920s while attending school in France. By 1934 he had returned to China and participated in the Long March. Nevertheless, his personal history did not shield him from Mao during the Cultural Revolution. Surprisingly, Deng reemerged from this disastrous decade and became China's preeminent leader from 1978 until the time of his death in 1997. Throughout his tenure, Deng remained committed to maintaining social stability. He also wanted to avoid the cult of the leader that Mao had engendered. Consequently, Deng rejected most official party positions, serving instead as the important chairman of the Central Military Commission. Despite his relative lack of titles, he was the de facto leader

Figure 8.1. Deng Xiaoping (Wikimedia Commons,
http://en.wikipedia.org/wiki/File:DengXiaoping.jpg.)

of China, and everybody, from the most isolated peasant to the party secretary, knew Deng was the man in charge. Just as he avoided formal titles, he also avoided ideological labels. "It does not matter if a cat is black or white," he explained, "as long as it catches mice."[2] Deng advocated pragmatic solutions to China's problems, promoting those ideas and individuals that could get the job done, regardless of party dogma. Most notably, he set out to modernize China in four separate areas: agriculture, industry, science, and the military.[3]

In the area of agriculture, Deng quickly broke up the massive communes throughout the country. Instead the government gave families small plots of land to control as they deemed appropriate. The "household responsibility system" allowed farmers to select (within limits) which crops they would grow and permitted them to sell any surplus on the free market. Technically the state still owned the land, and farmers were required to pay taxes on their produce. Nevertheless, the state suddenly played a much smaller role in the agricultural economy. Within a few short years, cash income quadrupled for the average farmer and starvation quickly became a forgotten crisis of earlier years.

Just as Deng hoped to modernize the economy, he believed a similar responsibility system would transform industrial productivity. He suggested separating ownership from management. The state would still own the factory, but business leaders would manage it free of government influence. Most profits would go to the state, but a percentage would stay with the company to be distributed or reinvested according to the wishes of professional managers. Again, as seen in the case of agriculture, industrial productivity steadily ticked upward. At the same time, Deng advocated the creation of Special Economic Zones. Within these zones, foreign investors could build factories and hire laborers with virtually no interference from the government. To encourage long-term investment, the party granted extended land-use permits ranging anywhere from a few months to dozens of years. Shenzhen, a small fishing village on China's southeast coast, was one such Special Economic Zone. Within a generation, its population exploded from a few thousand residents to over fourteen million, making it one of the largest cities in the world.

The modernization of science and technology proved to be especially difficult in the post-Mao era. Mao's emphasis on voluntarism—his faith in sheer willpower at the expense of expert skills—meant that many qualified scientists and technicians were marginalized in favor of individuals that may have been more politically acceptable but less educationally competent. Furthermore, the Cultural Revolution forced many universities to shut down, leading to a generation of undereducated students. The solution, Deng and others believed, was to send the

Figure 8.2. Shenzhen at night. (Wikimedia Commons, http://en.wikipedia.org/wiki/Shenzhen.)

best and brightest young men and women overseas to enroll in foreign universities. On graduating, they would return to China and become leaders in the areas of science and education.

Finally, Deng wanted to modernize the military. Rather than paying for a massive army, he suggested reducing the number of men in uniform and using the savings to invest in high-tech weaponry. China had already developed the nuclear bomb in 1964, but Deng wanted to add additional weapons such as nuclear submarines, intercontinental ballistic missiles, and fighter jets. Since 1978 China has dramatically increased its military budget and today has one of the most powerful armed forces in the world. In each of these four areas— agriculture, industry, science, and the military—Deng advocated pragmatic solutions to difficult problems. His goal was to create wealth for the Chinese people and garner international respect for the nation.

Tiananmen and the Fifth Modernization

In the 1978, Wei Jingsheng challenged the government to add one more item to its list of reforms. Without the fifth modernization, democracy, the other four were meaningless, Wei argued. Wei wrote his challenge on a large poster and affixed it on a public wall in downtown Beijing. An electrician at the Beijing Zoo, Wei was hardly the stereotypical rebel. Nevertheless, dozens of others followed Wei's lead and posted similar posters along the wall. The government responded by arresting Wei as a British spy and sentencing him to fifteen years in prison.[4]

Wei's arrest did not silence other democracy advocates, but they realized they had to be more circumspect in their methods. For the next decade, students and other intellectuals found creative ways to discuss democracy without directly challenging the party's right to rule. Many top officials, including Party General Secretary Hu Yaobang, responded favorably to talk of political reform. When Hu died in the spring of 1989, democracy advocates seized the opportunity. They gathered in Tiananmen Square ostensibly to mourn the death of Hu, but the gathering soon became an overt call for political reform. Led primarily by students from Beijing's various universities, the Tiananmen demonstration quickly escalated, with as many as one million individuals congregating in the square. It was a party-like atmosphere, with dancing, eating, and fraternizing. Students from the Central Academy of Fine Arts contributed to the environment by constructing a large "Goddess of Democracy," which looked uncannily like the Statue of Liberty, and erecting it in the square. When the government asked the students to leave, they refused, demanding that party leaders meet with them to discuss the future of the Chinese state. In addition to democratic reforms, the demonstrators wanted an end to corruption, economic liberalization, and greater government transparency.

For several weeks there appeared to be a stalemate between the party and the protestors. The crowds grew larger and larger, yet the government failed to respond in any way to their requests. To increase pressure, student leaders called

Figure 8.3: The Goddess of Democracy during the
Tiananmen demonstrations of 1989. (Wikimedia
Commons, http://en.wikipedia.org/wiki/
File:Tiananmen_square_protests_of_1989.jpg.).

on the demonstrators to engage in hunger strikes. Several hundred responded to
the call, and what had once been a party atmosphere quickly became much more
somber. Behind closed doors party leaders argued with one another about the
best course of action to follow.[5] In the end, the hardliners won out. Supported by
Deng Xiaoping, they called on the military to forcibly remove the students from
the square. During the early morning hours of 4 June, thousands of armed soldiers
fired on the crowds while tank drivers crushed their injured bodies. Within a few
hours, an eerie silence filled the square as the remnants of the protestors stole away
in the predawn darkness.

International observers speculate as many as three thousand protestors were
killed in the Tiananmen crackdown, though it is impossible to verify that number.
Today the government strictly censors any discussion of the Tiananmen protests
and refuses to allow a thorough investigation. Democracy, the fifth modernization,
was obviously not part of Deng Xiaoping's agenda for China.

CHINA'S HIGH-GROWTH ERA

In the immediate aftermath of the Tiananmen crackdown, China's economy went into a tailspin. International financiers feared political unrest would threaten their investments in China. Many predicted that political hard-liners would resume control over the party and reverse many of Deng's modernizing reforms. In short, China watchers from around the world stepped back to gauge the political winds in Beijing. In 1992 Deng Xiaoping made a very symbolic trip to southern China. Visiting the Special Economic Zone of Shenzhen, he repeatedly hailed the policies of economic reform, explaining that extreme "leftism" was a greater threat to China than was extreme "rightism." Everybody clearly understood the message: China was still open for business and would not return to the systems of the pre-Deng era.

Deng Xiaoping died of Parkinson's disease in 1997. His method of ruling from behind the scenes allowed for a relatively smooth transfer of power and a nearly seamless continuation of his policies. Since 1997 China has moved toward even greater economic liberalization under the unquestioned leadership of the Chinese Communist Party. Referred to as "socialism with Chinese characteristics," this model of development has caught the attention of the entire world. Free-market forces, guided by an authoritarian central regime, have allowed China to enjoy many years of high economic growth rates, ranging between 6 and 10 percent annually. According to the World Bank, in the twenty years following the death of Deng, China's gross domestic product increased nearly 13 fold, making it the second largest economy in the world behind only the United States.[6] It is among the most active international trading nations and has the world's largest foreign exchange reserves.[7] Perhaps most impressively, this economic growth has provided the average Chinese with greater purchasing power and pulled millions of people out of poverty. By the 2010s, less than 1.4% of the population lived below the absolute poverty line.[8] Not surprisingly, developing countries from Africa, Asia, and Latin America have studied the "China model," rejecting American-style political liberalism as too messy and inefficient. Even many Americans concede that China seems able to achieve remarkable economic goals with relative ease.

In the years since Deng's rise to power, government policies coupled with the hard work and creativity of ordinary people have created an extraordinary transformation. Many well-educated and cosmopolitan individuals have publicly supported the party's right to rule and rejected democracy, claiming it is unsuitable for China. Nationalism and economic growth are increasingly the raisons d'être of the party. Communist leaders routinely portray themselves as both economic engineers and as defenders of national pride. If incomes continue to rise and as long as China has perceived international critics, the party's grip on power appears secure.[9]

In many ways, Xi Jinping symbolizes this ongoing transformation. Born in 1953, Xi's life roughly corresponds with that of the People's Republic. The son of

Figure 8.4. Beijing Airport Terminal 3, constructed to accommodate traffic at the 2008 Olympics. (Wikimedia Commons, http://en.wikipedia.org/wiki/File:PEK_T3_1037.jpg.)

a communist party veteran, Xi was sent to the countryside during the Cultural Revolution. After the death of Mao, he slowly rose through the ranks of the party. Along the way he advocated economic development tempered by loyalty to communist officials. By 2013 he was named General Secretary of the Party and President of the People's Republic.

During his tenure, China became increasingly assertive in international affairs. This is perhaps best symbolized by the so-called "Belt and Road Initiative." With massive financial support from the central government, the Belt and Road Initiative includes Chinese investments in rail lines, port facilities, highways, and other such infrastructural projects to enhance trade and communication. Many of these ventures are in Africa, Southeast Asia, and other developing regions. By so doing, China hopes to create a twenty-first-century version of the ancient "Silk Road," with people and products moving across the world. The underlying goal for Xi and his like-minded supporters is the return of China to the top ranks of global power.

Of course, China still faces many real and serious challenges.[10] For instance, some nations welcome Chinese investment and international influence. Given its size, population, wealth, and history, it is only natural for China to play a large role in the global community. However, others are fearful of this trend. In 2016, US President Donald Trump rode a wave of populism into office, in large measure fueled by fears of an expansionist China. China's leaders need to employ creative diplomacy as they interact with their Washington counterparts who are eager to maintain American economic and military dominance.

One sticking point in US-China relations is the ongoing status of Taiwan, or the Nationalist remnants of the Republic of China. While President Nixon had begun the process of rapprochement with the People's Republic in 1972, it was left to his successor, Jimmy Carter, to complete this process. In 1979, Washington formally recognized the Chinese Communist regime as the legitimate government of China, and other countries around the world followed suit. At the same time, however, the US continues to sell military hardware to Taiwan. If either Beijing or Taiwan were to provoke a military confrontation, the US has left open the option to either intervene or to stand down. This intentional ambiguity on the part of Washington has, in part, led to Taiwan's state of limbo in the international arena.

Despite its pariah status, modern Taiwan has had many significant accomplishments. By the 1970s, the island state was well on its way to becoming an economic powerhouse in East Asia. During the 1980s, Taiwan's government leaders ended martial law after approximately four decades and instituted sweeping political reforms, including the creation of a multiparty democracy. While Beijing remains committed to Taiwan's eventual reunification with the mainland, Taiwan's residents increasingly see themselves as both culturally and politically distinct from China. Frequently Beijing uses military, economic, and legal tools to ratchet up the pressure on Taiwan, hoping to coerce or entice Taiwan's residents into the PRC fold. In nearly every instance, however, the majority of Taiwan's residents have responded by rejecting Beijing's overtures. For example, in 2020 individuals from across the island flocked to the polls to elect a new president. The two leading candidates were Tsai Ing-wen, a member of the Democratic Progressive Party and a harsh critic of Beijing. Her opponent was Han Kuo-yu, a member of the Nationalist Party and a proponent of improved relations with the mainland. Despite Beijing's attempts to influence the course of the election, Tsai won a lopsided victory.

Much like Taiwan, Hong Kong has proven to be an intractable challenge for Beijing as well. Following the Opium War of 1839-42, Hong Kong became a British colony. Fifty-six years later, in 1898, London coerced the Qing government into signing the Convention for the Extension of Hong Kong Territory, which enlarged the borders of the colony to include the so-called New Territories for a symbolic 99 years. Despite having a London-appointed governor, for most of its history Hong Kong benefited from what historians have called "benign neglect." Repeated waves of skilled, hardworking immigrants from China transformed the city from a modest fishing village to a major trading port, financial center, and industrial hub. In the 1980s, British officials announced that with the expiration of the 99-year lease on the New Territories, the entire colony would be returned to Chinese control. To earn the trust of Hong Kongers, Beijing announced the so-

Figure 8.5. Pandas in Chengdu's Breeding Research Base. Development and pollution have severely limited the panda's natural habitat, requiring intensive government intervention to protect the species. (Photo by author)

called "One Country, Two Systems" policy. Accordingly, Hong Kong would retain its own governmental, cultural, and financial systems for a period of at least 50 years, so long as it remained loyal to the Chinese state. In 1997, after 156 years of British rule, Hong Kong once again became part of China.

Since the handover, Beijing has largely honored the "One Country, Two Systems" policy. Nevertheless, the citizens in Hong Kong have become increasingly frustrated with Beijing's influence on the city. Rising real estate prices, stagnant wages, and the arrival of thousands of wealthy immigrants and tourists from the mainland have caused stress levels in Hong Kong to escalate. While Hong Kongers have been allowed a voice in selecting their government leaders, Beijing insists that candidates for office must first demonstrate their loyalty to China. Additionally, during the 2010s, some Hong Kong critics of Beijing inexplicably went missing, only to appear days later in China under police custody. In 2019, pro-China politicians in Hong Kong proposed a new extradition bill, which would allow for suspected criminals to be extradited to China to stand trial, thereby bypassing Hong Kong's independent judiciary. Almost immediately, Hong Kongers took to the streets in protest. The government soon backed down and rescinded the bill, but the crowds would not be pacified. Protests grew larger and larger, and the police responded with increasingly harsh measures, including tear gas and water cannons. Officials in Beijing realized that the situation was quickly getting out of hand, and in 2020 the National People's Congress approved the creation of a national security law, which would criminalize secession, subversion, terrorism, or any destabilizing foreign involvement in Hong Kong's affairs. Predictably, tensions between Hong Kong and Beijing remain fractious and severe.

Other domestic problems continue to vex party leaders in twenty-first century China. Although development has improved the lives of nearly all Chinese, there is greater income disparity now than any time since the 1949 revolution. The divide between the haves and have-nots roughly corresponds to the rural-urban divide. Cities along the east coast, such as Beijing, Tianjin, Shanghai, Shenzhen, and Guangzhou, have some of the highest per capita incomes in the nation. Modern apartment buildings, Internet access, and megamalls filled with shops are common in these locales. Many smaller villages in the interior, by contrast, are developmentally decades behind their urban counterparts. Many are without inside plumbing and electrification. Some even lack potable water. Predictably, millions of rural residents have migrated to the big cities along the coast in search of economic opportunity and a higher standard of living. Unfortunately, such migration is largely illegal within China. Therefore, migrants comprise an undocumented underclass performing those jobs most city dwellers refuse to do, including construction and assembly-line work and other labor-intensive tasks. Many of the migrants are young, single women. On arriving in the city, the average worker struggles with issues revolving around class, family, and gender while suffering from the effects of displacement and cultural dislocation.

Rapid economic development has also led to environmental degradation. The widespread use of coal-fired power plants creates a permanent haze over many Chinese cities. With increasing wealth, individuals are buying more and more automobiles, which only exacerbate the pollution problem. The party realizes this development model is unsustainable and has invested heavily in wind power, hydro power, and other forms of green energy. However, for the foreseeable future, China will be facing daunting environmental challenges.

Precisely because it has been so impressive, economic development may have created expectations that are unrealistic over the long term. China's many years of high growth rates have defied the predictions of numerous well-respected economists, and many suggest that the economy is not as solid as it might first appear. Labor unrest, inflation, trade wars, and a restrictive financial system all have the potential to negatively impact China's economy. Coupled with the lack of a welfare safety net, an economic slowdown could lead to social and political instability. Trade wars and global pandemics have highlighted the potential shortcomings of China's economic development model.

Additional noneconomic problems have the potential to destabilize the Communist Party. Because it is a large multiethnic state, Chinese political leaders must find ways to satisfy its large non-Chinese population. Tibetans and Uighurs, in particular, must be persuaded to feel a sense of belonging within the

Figure 8.6. Pilgrims and tourists circumambulating the sacred Jokhang Temple in Lhasa, Tibet. (Photo by author.)

People's Republic. Some party leaders believe this should be accomplished by placing individuals with suspect loyalties in re-education camps. Others argue that granting these groups greater autonomy is the solution. Still others believe that by encouraging ethnic Chinese to migrate to Tibetan and Uighur regions these peoples will be culturally assimilated. The 2008 protests in Tibet, the 2009 Uighur riots, the 2011 Inner Mongolian demonstrations, the 2012 surge of self-immolations in Tibet, and the 2018 detention of perhaps 1 million Uighurs all suggest that ethnic tension remains a difficult problem for China's political elite, and the international community follows these developments with great interest.

Despite these challenges, the Chinese Communist Party benefits from the support and trust of many of its citizens. The pragmatic, pro-growth policies implemented since 1976 have allowed the Chinese to achieve higher standards of living than ever before, without the social chaos and ongoing revolution of the earlier Mao Zedong era. Though many problems continue to exist, the average Chinese citizen enjoys material and social benefits that were inconceivable a few short years ago.

The story of modern China involves a wide cast of characters, fully engaged with the larger world through cross-cultural encounters. It is an exceptional story, but with many familiar themes that can and should be understood by all students

st century. From peasants to Red Guards to China's new ardent
d women from all segments of society have influenced modern
ul, undoubtedly, continue to shape the future for both China and

NOTES

CHAPTER 1

[1] E. Backhouse and J. O. P. Bland, *Annals and Memoirs of the Court of Peking* (Boston: Houghton Mifflin, 1914), 322–31, quoted at http://academic.brooklyn. cuny.edu/core9/phalsall/texts/qianlong.html (accessed July 12, 2012).

CHAPTER 2

[1] Immanuel C. Y. Hsu, *The Rise of Modern China* (New York: Oxford University Press, 2000), 168.

[2] S. Y. Teng and John K. Fairbank, *China's Response to the West: A Documentary Survey, 1839–1923* (Cambridge: Harvard University Press, 1954), 24–27, quoted in Hsu, The Rise of Modern China, 180.

CHAPTER 3

[1] Richard J. Smith, *China's Cultural Heritage: The Qing Dynasty, 1644–1912* (Boulder: Westview Press, 1994), 74–75.

[2] Ichisada Miyazaki, *China's Examination Hell: The Civil Service Examinations of Imperial China* (New York: Weatherhill, 1976), 16.

[3] Shawn Ni and Pham Hoang Van, "High Corruption Income in Ming and Qing China," *Journal of Development Economics*, vol. 81 (December 2006).

[4] Jonathan D. Spence, *Death of Woman Wang* (New York: Penguin, 1998).

[5] Ramon H. Myers and Yeh-Chien Wang, "Economic Developments, 1644–1800," in *The Cambridge History of China*, vol. 9, The Ch'ing Empire to 1800, edited by Willard Peterson, 643–44 (Cambridge: Cambridge University Press, 2002).

[6] Jonathan D. Spence, *God's Chinese Son: The Taiping Heavenly Kingdom of Hong Xiuquan* (New York: W. W. Norton, 1996).

[7] Samir Amin, "Forerunners of the Contemporary World: The Paris Commune (1871) and the Taiping Revolution (1851–1864)," *International Critical Thought*, 3.2 (2013): 159-164.

CHAPTER 4

[1] For more information on the Beiyang Fleet and China's naval development, see John Lang Rawlinson, *China's Struggle for Naval Development, 1839–1895* (Cambridge, Mass.: Harvard University Press, 1967).

[2] Hu Shi, "Yung Wing," *Chinese Studies in History* 35.3 (Spring 2002): 87–96.

[3] Hsiao Kung-ch'uan, *A Modern China and a New World: K'ang Yu-wei, Reformer and Utopian, 1858–1927* (Seattle: University of Washington Press, 1975).

[4] For more information on the Boxer Rebellion, see Paul A. Cohen, *History in Three Keys: The Boxers as Event, Experience, and Myth* (New York: Columbia University Press, 1997).

[5] According to many sources, German troops were most prone to committing atrocities, whereas the Japanese and American troops displayed the most restraint and discipline.

[6] This view, first expressed by Sir Edmund Backhouse, influenced generations of China scholars. See J. O. P. Bland and Edmund Backhouse, *China under the Empress Dowager: Being the History of the Life and Times of Tzu Hsi, Comp. from the State Papers of the Comptroller of Her Household* (Boston: Houghton Mifflin, 1914).

[7] See, for instance, Sterling Seagrave and Peggy Seagrave, *Dragon Lady: The Life and Legend of the Last Empress of China* (New York: Knopf, 1992).

CHAPTER 5

[1] Marie-Claire Bergère and Janet Lloyd, *Sun Yat-Sen* (Stanford, Calif.: Stanford University Press, 1998).

[2] Jerome Ch'en, *Yuan Shih-K'ai* (Stanford, Calif.: Stanford University Press, 1972).

[3] Chen Duxiu, "Xin qingnian zuian zhi dabianshu" [*New Youth*'s reply to charges against the magazine], *Xin Qingnian* (New Youth), 6.1 (15 January 1919): 10-11, quoted in Edward X. Gu, "Who Was Mr. Democracy? The May Fourth Discourse of Populist Democracy and the Radicalization of Chinese Intellectuals (1915-1922)," *Modern Asian Studies* 35.3 (2001): 589.

[4] Kai-wing Chow, *Beyond the May Fourth Paradigm: In Search of Chinese Modernity* (Lanham, MD.: Lexington Books and Rowman & Littlefield, 2008).

[5] Jay Taylor, *The Generalissimo: Chiang Kai-shek and the Struggle for Modern China* (Cambridge, Mass.: Belknap Press of Harvard University Press, 2009).

[6] Frederic E. Wakeman and Richard L. Edmonds, *Reappraising Republican China* (Oxford: Oxford University Press, 2000).

CHAPTER 6

[1] Diana Lary, *The Chinese People at War: Human Suffering and Social Transformation, 1937–1945* (Cambridge: Cambridge University Press, 2010).

[2] Prasenjit Duara, *Sovereignty and Authenticity: Manchukuo and the East Asian Modern* (Lanham, Md.: Rowman and Littlefield, 2003); Shin'ichi Yamamuro and Joshua A. Fogel, *Manchuria under Japanese Dominion* (Philadelphia: University of Pennsylvania Press, 2006).

[3] Joshua A. Fogel, *The Nanjing Massacre in History and Historiography* (Berkeley: University of California Press, 2000).

[4] David P. Barrett and Lawrence N. Shyu, *Chinese Collaboration with Japan, 1932– 1945: The Limits of Accommodation* (Stanford, Calif.: Stanford University Press, 2001); Timothy Brook, *Collaboration: Japanese Agents and Local Elites in Wartime China* (Cambridge, Mass.: Harvard University Press, 2005).

[5] Eri Hotta, *Pan-Asianism and Japan's War, 1931–1945* (New York: Palgrave Macmillan, 2007).

[6] Taylor, *The Generalissimo: Chiang Kai-shek and the Struggle for Modern China.*

[7] Rana Mitter, *Forgotten Ally: China's World War II, 1937–1945* (New York: Houghton Mifflin, 2013); Taylor, *The Generalissimo: Chiang Kai-shek and the Struggle for Modern China*; and Parks M. Coble, *China's War Reporters: The Legacy of Resistance against Japan* (Cambridge: Harvard University Press, 2015).

[8] John W. Dower, *Embracing Defeat: Japan in the Wake of World War II* (New York: W. W. Norton, 1999), 49.

[9] Wen-Hsin Yeh, *Provincial Passages: Culture, Space, and the Origins of Chinese Communism* (Berkeley: University of California Press, 1996); Tony Saich and Hans J. Van de Ven, *New Perspectives on the Chinese Communist Revolution* (Armonk, N.Y.: M. E. Sharpe, 1995); Tony Saich, *The Rise to Power of the Chinese Communist Party: Documents and Analysis* (Armonk, N.Y.: M. E. Sharpe, 1993).

[10] Governments and demographers offer widely diverging estimates of war casualties, including both military and collateral deaths. During the war with Japan, estimates range between ten and twenty million. During the ensuing civil war, estimates range between one and three million, the majority of which were Guomindang losses.

CHAPTER 7

[1] Xianhui Yang, *The Woman from Shanghai*, trans. Wen Huang (New York: Pantheon Books, 2009).

[2] Frederick C. Teiwes and Warren Sun, *China's Road to Disaster: Mao, Central Politicians, and Provincial Leaders in the Unfolding of the Great Leap Forward, 1955–1959* (Armonk, N.Y.: M.E. Sharpe, 1999).

[3] Andrew G. Walder, *Fractured Rebellion: The Beijing Red Guard Movement* (Cambridge, Mass.: Harvard University Press, 2009).

[4] Timothy Cheek, ed., *A Critical Introduction to Mao* (Cambridge: Cambridge University Press, 2010).

[5] Yang Su, *Collective Killings in Rural China during the Cultural Revolution* (Cambridge: Cambridge University Press, 2011).

CHAPTER 8

[1] Ezra F. Vogel, *Deng Xiaoping and the Transformation of China* (Cambridge, Mass.: Belknap Press of Harvard University Press, 2011).

[2] Deng reportedly first uttered this phrase in 1962, before the Cultural Revolution. It is an old Sichuan Province proverb.

[3] Richard Baum, *China's Four Modernizations: The New Technological Revolution* (Boulder: Westview Press, 1980).

[4] Wei Jingsheng and Kristina M. Torgeson, *The Courage to Stand Alone: Letters from Prison and Other Writings* (New York: Viking, 1997).

[5] Zhang Liang, Andrew J. Nathan, and E. P. Link, *The Tiananmen Papers* (New York: Public Affairs, 2001).

[6] World Bank data as accessed through Google Public Data Explorer, https://www.google.com/publicdata/directory (last accessed 12 September 2018).

[7] *CIA World Factbook 2011*, China, https://www.cia.gov/library/publications/theworld-factbook/geos/ch.html (accessed 8 August 2011).

[8] The World Bank Poverty and Equity Data Portal: China, http://povertydata.worldbank.org/poverty/country/CHN (accessed 12 September 2018).

[9] David C. Kang, *China Rising: Peace, Power, and Order in East Asia* (New York: Columbia University Press, 2007).

[10] Susan L. Shirk, *China: Fragile Superpower* (Oxford: Oxford University Press, 2007).

GLOSSARY

Belt and Road Initiative. A policy unveiled in 2013 and directed from Beijing. It seeks to improve overland and maritime transport routes with the goals of enhancing international trade and increasing Chinese global influence. As part of this initiative, Beijing invested heavily in rail lines, ports, and roads throughout Africa, Asia, and even Europe.

Boxers. Groups of men in late-nineteenth-century China who practiced martial arts or "Chinese boxing." Frustrated by their lack of economic opportunities, some of these groups began attacking foreigners and Chinese Christians. These actions precipitated the so-called Boxer Rebellion in 1900.

Canton system. A system designed by the Qing dynasty rulers to control and manage trade with the West. The system was centered on the southeastern city of Guangzhou (Canton).

Civil servant. An individual who earned his bureaucratic position by passing the civil service examination. Such exams were common from the time of the Song dynasty (960–1279) and continued through the Qing dynasty (1644–1912).

Commune. A large agricultural complex established in the 1950s to pool agricultural resources and increase production during the Great Leap Forward.

Deng Xiaoping. China's paramount leader from 1978 to 1997. Deng advocated a pragmatic rather than an ideological approach to economic development.

Exceptionalism. The belief that China does not conform to widely-accepted norms or patterns followed by other nation-states.

Extraterritoriality. First introduced by the British following the Opium War, this concept held that British citizens traveling and residing in China were not subject to Chinese law. Any legal proceeding involving a British subject was handled by British authorities. By the end of the nineteenth century, most Western nations and Japan had gained the right of extraterritoriality in China.

Foot binding. The practice of binding a young girl's feet to keep them from growing naturally. It was believed this would form a more attractive foot and enhance a woman's social position.

Gentry. The wealthy, scholarly elite who assisted the official civil servants in administering local affairs.

Great Leap Forward. The attempt to dramatically increase China's industrial and agricultural productivity during the 1950s. An estimated thirty million Chinese starved in large part because of the disastrous policies of the Great Leap Forward.

Greater East Asia Co-Prosperity Sphere. The term used by Tokyo to describe those areas conquered by Japanese troops in the 1940s.

Gunboat diplomacy. The use of military force by foreign powers to extract diplomatic concessions from the Qing dynasty.

Informal imperialism. The policy of securing imperialist privileges in China without formally annexing Chinese territory. *See also* "gunboat diplomacy."

Kangxi. Reign name of the Manchu emperor of China from 1661 to 1722. Considered one of China's greatest rulers, he exemplified skill and dexterity in dealing with Russians, Jesuits, and Chinese.

Manchukuo. The term used by Tokyo to describe the puppet state of Manchuria in Northeast China between 1931 and 1945.

Manchus. The ethnic group from Manchuria in Northeast China. The Manchus established the Qing dynasty in 1644 and governed China until 1912.

Mao Zedong. Leader of the People's Republic of China from its founding in 1949 until his death in 1976. Credited with the successful Communist Revolution but blamed for the disastrous Great Leap Forward and Cultural Revolution, Mao's legacy remains hotly debated to the present day.

New Culture Movement. A period of cultural questioning and reform that lasted from approximately 1915 to 1925. Students and faculty from Peking University were the primary advocates of the New Culture Movement.

Official Qing cosmology. The worldview that posits China as the Middle Kingdom surrounded by peoples of varying degrees of civilization and barbarity. All interactions between China and the larger world were to be predicated on this assumption.

One Country, Two Systems. A policy announced by Beijing for the governing of Hong Kong in which the city retains many of its own political, financial, and educational systems for a period of at least 50 years following the end of British colonial rule in 1997.

Prefectures. Under the leadership of the Communist Party, China was divided into approximately thirty-three provinces, with each province consisting of numerous prefectures. Today there are over three hundred prefectures in China.

Qianlong. Manchu emperor of China from 1735 to 1796, Qianlong was the grandson of the illustrious Kangxi emperor. Like his grandfather, Qianlong continued the tradition of fostering Chinese culture while maintaining control over a multiethnic empire.

Rape of Nanjing. An approximately six-week period in late 1937 and early 1938 during which Japanese troops, after seizing the Chinese city of Nanjing, engaged in wanton rape, murder, and torture. As many as three hundred thousand Chinese were killed during this incident.

Self-Strengthening Movement. The late-nineteenth-century attempt to reform and modernize China under government direction.

Sun Yat-sen. Leader of the 1911 revolution that brought an end to the Qing dynasty. Sun hoped to create a democratic republic, but at the time of his death in 1925 China was fragmented into warring states.

Syndicalism. An economic system that privileges the input of labor unions in making economic and political decisions. Syndicalism was a popular concept in early-twentieth-century China and facilitated the spread of communist ideology among China's intellectuals.

Taipings. Followers of Hong Xiuquan, a spiritual leader of the mid– nineteenth century who unsuccessfully attempted to overthrow the Qing dynasty and establish a theocracy.

Total war. The use of all available material and human resources, total war can also refer to attitudes and behavior. For example, some claim that normal rules of engagement and expectations of ethical, moral treatment are unrealistic during periods of total war and therefore nations and individuals have unrestricted authority to inflict terror and destroy the enemy.

United front. Refers to one of two attempts by the Nationalist Party and the Communist Party to cooperate in a common goal. The first united front was in the 1920s and sought to overthrow the various warlords in China. The second was in the 1930s and 1940s and sought to expel the Japanese invaders from China.

Xi Jinping. The paramount leader of the Chinese state after ascending to the post of General Secretary of the Communist Party in November 2012. He was also named the Chairman of the Central Military Commission and President of the People's Republic of China. A charismatic and driven leader, Xi wielded greater influence than any Chinese leader since Deng Xiaoping in the 1990s.

Suggestions for Further Reading

Atwill, David G., and Yurong Y. Atwill. *Sources in Chinese History: Diverse Perspectives from 1644 to the Present*. Upper Saddle River, N.J.: Pearson and Prentice Hall, 2010.

Becker, Jasper. *The Chinese*. New York: Free Press, 2000.

Bianco, Lucien. *Origins of the Chinese Revolution, 1915–1949*. Stanford, Calif.: Stanford University Press, 1971.

Crossley, Pamela Kyle. *The Wobbling Pivot, China since 1800: An Interpretive History*. Chichester, West Sussex: Wiley-Blackwell, 2010.

Dirlik, Arif. *The Origins of Chinese Communism*. New York: Oxford University Press, 1989.

Duara, Prasenjit. *Rescuing History from the Nation: Questioning Narratives of Modern China*. Chicago: University of Chicago Press, 1995.

Ebrey, Patricia Buckley. *The Cambridge Illustrated History of China*. Cambridge: Cambridge University Press, 1996.

———. *Chinese Civilization and Society: A Sourcebook*. New York: Free Press, 1981.

Elvin, Mark. *The Pattern of the Chinese Past: A Social and Economic Interpretation*. Stanford, Calif.: Stanford University Press, 1973.

Fairbank, John King. *The Great Chinese Revolution, 1800–1985*. New York: Harper and Row, 1986.

Fairbank, John King, and Merle Goldman. *China: A New History*. Cambridge, Mass.: Belknap Press of Harvard University Press, 1998.

Harrison, Henrietta. *China*. London: Arnold, 2001.

Hutchings, Graham. *Modern China: A Guide to a Century of Change*. Cambridge, Mass.: Harvard University Press, 2001.

Hsü, Immanuel C. Y. *The Rise of Modern China*. New York: Oxford University Press, 1970.

Rawski, Evelyn Sakakida. *The Last Emperors: A Social History of Qing Imperial Institutions*. Berkeley: University of California Press, 1998.

Rowe, William T. *China's Last Empire: The Great Qing*. Cambridge, Mass.: Belknap Press of Harvard University Press, 2009.

Saich, Tony, and Hans J. Van de Ven. *New Perspectives on the Chinese Communist Revolution*. Armonk, N.Y.: M. E. Sharpe, 1995.

Schoppa, R. Keith. *The Columbia Guide to Modern Chinese History*. New York: Columbia University Press, 2000.

———. *Revolution and Its Past: Identities and Change in Modern Chinese History*. Upper Saddle River, N.J.: Pearson Prentice Hall, 2006.

Spence, Jonathan D. *The Search for Modern China*. New York: Norton, 1990.

Tanner, Harold Miles. *China: A History*. Indianapolis: Hackett, 2009.

Tong, Scott. *A Village with My Name: A Family History of China's Opening to the World*. Chicago, University of Chicago Press, 2017.

Taylor, Jay. *The Generalissimo: Chiang Kai-shek and the Struggle for Modern China*. Cambridge, Mass.: Belknap Press of Harvard University Press, 2009.

Vogel, Ezra F. *Deng Xiaoping and the Transformation of China*. Cambridge, Mass.: Belknap Press of Harvard University Press, 2011.

Wang, Zheng. *Never Forget National Humiliation: Historical Memory in Chinese Politics and Foreign Relations*. New York: Columbia University Press, 2014.

Wasserstrom, Jeffrey N. *China in the Twenty-First Century: What Everyone Needs to Know*. New York: Oxford University Press, 2010.

———. *The Oxford Illustrated History of Modern China*. Oxford: Oxford University Press, 2016.

Zhu, Zhiqun. *China*. Boston: McGraw-Hill Higher Education, 2010.

CPSIA information can be obtained
at www.ICGtesting.com
Printed in the USA
LVHW041421130920
665725LV00001BA/5